S.A.I.L. Above the Clouds 2

How to ALIGN Your Life

A sailor's lessons for navigating challenges, mastering emotions, and harnessing personal power

First Edition

Book #2 of the S.A.I.L. Series: Simplify, Align, Integrate, Let Go ™

Carole Dion Fontaine

Inspired
CREATIONS
LLC

Copyright © 2023 by Carole D. Fontaine

All rights reserved. No part of this book may be reproduced in any form or by any electronic or mechanical means, including information storage and retrieval system, without prior written permission from the publisher, except by reviewers, who may quote brief passages in reviews or articles. For permission requests, write to the publisher at the address below.

Disclaimer: Carole Fontaine is a certified Life Coach. Tips and techniques in this book are offered as tools for a healthier and happier lifestyle. Please refer to a therapist or health care specialist for personal or medical challenges you may be experiencing.

ISBN 978-1-7361506-2-7 (Paperback Edition)
ISBN 978-1-7361506-3-4 (Ebook Edition)

Library of Congress Control Number: 2023920541

First Edition, 2023.

Editing: Sopurkha Kaur (Awareness Generation)

Cover and Book Design: Carole D. Fontaine

All Photographs © Carole D. Fontaine

Published by Inspired Creations, LLC
31 Rainbow Road
Shapleigh, ME 04076

sailabovetheclouds.com

Printed in the United States of America.

"May you flow through life with ease and grace."
—*Carole Fontaine*

Table of Contents

Acknowledgments	6
Preface	7
How to get the most out of S.A.I.L. ABOVE THE CLOUDS 2	9
A = Align your Life	13
1. Lightning Strikes—Two Sailors Meet Align with Possibilities	15
2. Divers Down—Fishing for Live Ones Align your Survival Instinct	27
3. James Bond's Cave—On a Mission to Glee Align your Actions with Joy	43
4. A Shitty Day—Kills the Mood Align with Authenticity	57
5. Dancing in the Galley—The Circle of Life Align your Timing	69
6. When Stuck—Save the Popsicles Align Patience with Positivity	81
7. Night Navigation—Blinded I Seek Align Actions with Intuition	93
8. Sailor's Fashion—Stop Judging my Flip-Flops Align Compassion with Humanity	107
9. Salty Goodbyes—Spirit Voyage Align with the Divine	123
10. Resist the Elements—Dinghy Mishap Align Decisions with Mindfulness	135
11. Magic Underway—A Reiki Sail Align your Chakras	147

12. An Empty Rum Barrel—A Pirate on the Ratlines Align Boundaries and Respect	159
13. Shine On—Finding My Treasure Align your Motivation with Passion	171
14. Orgasmic Stars—Riding the Big One Align your Shakti Energy	181
15. Detours—Close Call with a Sea Monster Align Feelings and Emotions	193
16. Provisioning Tale—A Soda Trail Align with Flexibility	203
17. Furbaby—My Salty Tail Align your Tail with Wisdom	213
18. Love Thy Engine—Diesel & Spine Align your Body	221
19. Feast on Self-Love—For Gut's Sake Align Nutrition and your Gut	227
20. Three Sheets to the Wind—A Rebel Crew Align Communications with your Heart	235
Conclusion Align with Purpose	247
Sneak Peek Book #3	252
What's Ahead?	253
FREEBIES	256
About The Author	257
References & Resources	258
Journaling	260

Acknowledgments

To my beloved Eric, thank you for navigating this wild life with me. We're not done yet, so don't let go! I love you.

To the sisterhood of women seekers, dreamers, and lovers who share your light and serve—may you stay bright, stay true, and keep your hearts aligned with spirit.

To the men who love and support these women to discover what ignites their souls—thank you for encouraging them to share it with the world.

To my amazing family and tribe of friends and supporters—thank you for carrying me through doubts and inspiring me to keep writing.

To all who may feel unseen, unheard, unsupported, comfortably numb, or lost in the drift—may you find your spark and light up the world.

Never stop seeking. Never stop growing. Never stop expanding.

"May the light of a thousand suns shine through.
Live the life of grace that you were meant to."
—GuruGanesha Band with Paloma Devi, A Thousand Suns

Preface

My baptism at sea came at the age of 29. You could say it's where a new chapter began. One filled with dreams of sailing the world, finding long-lost treasures, exploring deserted beaches, and living off the grid.

While it may not have unfolded exactly the way my husband and I had planned, our sailing journey ended up being exactly what was needed to shape us into stronger, braver, more resilient humans. We learned to grow, trust, and more deeply connect with ourselves, each other, and the world around us.

As our journey continued, I became more adept at handling Windsong, our 15-ton sailing vessel, and more comfortable in navigating this environment of facing ordeals and adapting more fluidly to situations. I developed a keen awareness of how the elements affected our sail and reflected on how the same could be said of our personal lives.

Resistance could be either the greatest obstacle or the ultimate guide—depending on my perspective and how open I was to course corrections, change of plans, or surprised groundings.

I observed how magnificent it was to surf the elements when all was in perfect alignment, right timing, and an inner compass guiding me to flow without resistance.

If I could master Windsong, could I apply its lessons to heal my body, my mind, my relationships and flow through life with as much ease and grace?

Our lives had taken a beating after years of chronic illness and I was ready to leave pain behind. I tasted the ocean on my lips and was reminded that saltiness ran through my veins and gave me life. We were connected, the ocean and I, bound by evolution, breathing the same air, and carrying similar unexplored depths.

If I could tap into even an ounce of my hidden potential, it would expand my possibilities, heighten my intuition, and guide me back to alignment.

The ocean taught me to be mindful. Sailing taught me to observe and trust my gut and to align my timing and energies with the ebb and flow of the world. Everything in life is intrinsically connected. By learning to recognize the threads and read the patterns around me I could weave a tapestry of my dreams.

There will always be daunting storms, strange encounters, and scary dives, but mastering my inner compass helped reveal a treasure much more precious than gold, it emblazoned my spirit with purpose.

It is with that spirit that I welcome you aboard, dear reader!

Whether you are on your maiden voyage with me or have previously sailed through Book 1, I dub thee an honorary crewmember of Windsong. Cut the lines, raise your sails, and kick off your shoes (or flip-flops). This is going to be a fun adventure—setting sail to search for your pearls of wisdom and discover what sets your soul on fire.

May my trials and tribulations inspire laughs, love, and insights.

Shine on!
Om Shanti, Namaste, Sat Nam,
Fair winds and following seas,

Carole Dion Fontaine *(Nam Karan Kaur)*
S/v Windsong

Align Your Life

How to get the most out of S.A.I.L. ABOVE THE CLOUDS 2

S.A.I.L. Above the Clouds is a series of four books, each filled with stories and adventures from my 20 years of living on a sailboat with my husband and our dog. Although the stories are not necessarily linear, I encourage you to start with book #1 of *S.A.I.L. Above the Clouds—How to Simplify Your Life* in order to get the full experience, gaining clarity and insights. You will also benefit from learning the history that builds on each book. However, *SAIL Above the Clouds 2—How to Align Your Life* can certainly be read as a stand-alone book.

Each book represents an aspect and a letter in my S.A.I.L.™ program, designed to help you:

    S = Simplify your life
    A = Align to Shine
    I = Integrate tools for success
    L = Let go of what doesn't serve you

…so you can create an extraordinary life (and sail above the clouds)!

Each chapter contains:

ADVENTURE: Salty tales and adventures.

LESSON: The lesson I learned.

QUESTION: A journaling prompt to promote self-awareness.

(A journaling section has been provided for you at the end of the book.)

You have deep wisdom inside of you that is untapped or blocked behind unconscious limiting beliefs. Journaling is a powerful tool that can give you great insights into how to heal and better your life. Answer the writing prompts as honestly as you can, with the first thought that comes to mind. It is imperative that you do not edit—use only these first thoughts, no matter how embarrassing or shocking they may be.

First thoughts have tremendous power and come directly from an unedited source, before our mind restricts, confines, judges, or polishes them. It is essential to air out these thoughts to:

1) Clear out your mind,
2) Remove/reduce the power these thoughts may have on you,
3) Discover what truly is at the source of your blockages,
4) Tap into your inner wisdom to improve your life,
5) Formulate a plan to reach your goals.

This practice will help you notice, understand, and change detrimental behaviors, habits, or negative self-talk. It can be exceptionally healing and life-changing if you allow it. Trust in the process. Be compassionate and allow yourself to let anything come up without judgment.

Take it one step further by setting up a timer for 5 minutes and write continuously until the bell rings. Do not stop or allow yourself time to think about your answer. You may surprise yourself with the words that pour out of you. Do not reread, cross out, or bother with grammar. Just write, uninterrupted, for 5 minutes or more. If you do not know what to write, simply write, "I don't know what to write." until something comes to mind, or the time is up. It is part of the process to work on the resistance you may feel on certain subjects.

 ACTION: A simple exercise to increase mindfulness, success, and promote a healthy lifestyle.

I challenge you to try these exercises. With courage and honesty, you might be surprised at how beneficial they can be in healing and finding your purpose.

When we SIMPLIFY our lives, our pathways and solutions become clear. We can then ALIGN and shine in all endeavors, INTEGRATE tools for success, and LET GO of fears and blockages, to fully embody our dreams.

My ultimate goal is to show you that no matter what ails you or what situation you face, you can meet it with a clear mind, and move past obstacles with a peaceful heart. My hope is you'll feel free to speak your truth, create flourishing relationships, pursue your dreams with passion, and embody health and success—no matter what life throws at you. Give yourself permission to go on this treasure hunt. This may be the greatest adventure you'll ever take!

MEDITATION DOWNLOAD: Each of the four books includes one free meditation available to download at sailabovetheclouds.com

I cannot praise the benefits of meditation enough. It is a daily time investment that will help you realize your goals. Think of meditation as exercising your brain muscles. Science agrees that having a mindfulness practice will not only raise your quality of life but can also extend it. People who meditate see their creativity improve, feel more relaxed, and reduce symptoms of stress, anxiety, and depression.

A John Hopkins study proved that meditation rivaled the effects of anti-depressants [1], while UCLA showed evidence that long-term meditators have better-preserved brains as they aged. [2] A study at Yale University proved that meditation does in fact allow individuals to be more present and aware, so they have better focus and a clearer, calmer mind [3].

Just imagine you are exploring your personal inner ocean.
Sail on sailor!

Book #1, ***SAIL Above the Clouds—How to Simplify Your Life***, was a Bestseller on Amazon for weeks, a finalist for Book of the Year from Book Talk Radio Club (UK), and sold copies across five continents!!

"Carole's book does a fantastic job of inspiring people to live a fulfilled life...I highly suggest it to our readers."
—Mike Desimon, SAIL JUNKY Magazine

"I am a therapist and a sailor! ...It is now a must-read for my clients! Loved it!"
—Shauna Hoffman, MA, MFT, Host Journey to Awareness

"Carole's book S.A.I.L. showcases the resiliency and adaptability needed to tackle the unpredictable nature of the sea and draws powerful parallels to the challenges faced in our everyday lives. Through her journey from being a novice to mastering the art of sailing a 20-ton boat, in addition to figuring out her own health issues, she serves as a beacon of strength and empowerment. ...inspire readers to confront their fears and embrace challenges... A truly uplifting and empowering writer (and human being)."
—Carolyn Delaney, Publisher, JOURNEY Magazine

"She's a package full of energy," and "...so inspiring," "...really amazing!"
—Paul Castronovo's BIG 105.9 FM Miami's #1 Rock Station

"A true-life story about a couple that made the decision to dramatically change their lives by buying, then moving aboard, a sailboat. Carole's "life lesson" is to simplify your values, and this book is an excellent example of how. Choosing to sail above the clouds is not a dreamer's quest; it is a survival skill."
—LATITUDES AND ATTITUDES Magazine

A = ALIGN YOUR LIFE

a·lign: to bring into line or alignment.

The second step to S.A.I.L.™ Above the Clouds is ALIGN.

If you know a little about sailboats or if you're a sailor, you know how every sail is a constant search for the perfect sail.

There are days when everything is in perfect alignment, and you feel like you're flying on air. The current, wind, angles, waves heights, and directions all support your goal, and you feel like everything is possible, you are the master of your domain, and nothing stands in the way of your synchronous flow with the universe. You are on top of the world!

The rest of the days are a search to reach that high and some of those days are flat out windless and deflated.

No matter where you are going, we're always in pursuit of that perfect path where all doors are opened, and opportunities arise in perfect synchronicity to support our lives and goals.

How we align every aspect of our lives, tweak our habits, nurture our energy, inspire our days, read the signs, and align our actions, with our heart, and spirit matters. It makes them exponentially more powerful and creates a great impact on our lives.

If you want to shine, align.

These are the lessons I learned that helped me along the way.

1. Lightning Strikes—Two Sailors Meet

Align with Possibilities

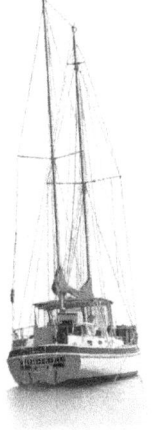

"Find what fuels your heart and light a match" —Carole

There was only one motorcycle helmet on top of the bar that night and it was mine. All 117 pounds of me rode in from out of town where I now lived—in the "big city" of Montreal where I finished art school and stayed to work as a graphic designer. I was back in my old stomping grounds for my mother's birthday but because I had worked overtime, I couldn't make it home before her bedtime. I'd decided to catch up with my high school girlfriends at the local watering hole.

It was a rough bar. My mother would not have approved. For a while, this hotel/motel had been a sleazy strip club, and eventually became the new venue for live bands. It was 1989 when screaming big hair, heavily glossed lips, and smoothly fitted black leather roamed all edges of that dance floor in rural East Farnham, population 500, in the middle of nowhere.

The bar was packed, triumphantly overcrowded for the show. Aromas swirled—smoke, stale beer, sweat, and overly perfumed young bodies high on raging hormones and illegal substances. Everyone was vying for the prized best-view landscape, pumping fists, shaking hips, and tapping boots to the beat of rock'n roll music.

The glam-rock band jammed everyone's favorites. Electric guitar so prominent it made the hair on our arms stand up. You could feel the loud beat of the drum, even see it ripple in your cocktail. A huge party scene, despite its tiny room, with people belting lyrics at the top of their lungs, dancing, and ordering copious amounts of alcohol.

We could barely hear our own words but at 21 years old, loud music made me feel alive. I lived for freedom and rock'n roll.

I heard the rumble of a motorcycle outside and instantly knew that a Harley Davidson "hog" had rolled in. "Loud pipes save lives," as their motto says, they also announce your arrival no matter how loud the environment is. I was curious to see who it was after developing my fascination for anything on two wheels. Ah-ha! I spotted him as he opened the door, his nose, and cheeks all rosy from riding the cold night. He was by himself—and insanely attractive.

He knew there was another motorhead in the bar since he'd parked next to my red Suzuki GS 550. Even though the place was packed, his searching eyes landed on my helmet sitting on the bar. He seemed to glide over as he zoned in on me, his eyes registering surprise when he realized that the biker, standing in leathers next to that helmet, was a girl. After locking eyes for half a second, I quickly looked away, faking disinterest, and laughed with my girlfriends.

"A girl?!" He thought. Not many women rode back in the late eighties, especially when fall rolled in and the nights became so chilled that it was necessary to wear full gear or fear purple fingers and toes, and frozen thighs. I was a biker, held my own, and loved the freedom of the road. It attracted some stares, and not always the flattering kind. But between art school, my purple hair phase (three decades before it would become fashionable), and motorcycling, I was used to pushing boundaries and reaping the judgments of others.

I stood out. He was attracted to my rebel spirit – and probably the tight leathers as well! It didn't take long before he maneuvered himself between my girlfriend and me, then asked me to dance. He had this air like he owned the place, half expecting I'd fall into his arms. I thought he was full of himself. He didn't even introduce himself and cut right into our conversation. Cute, yes, but no manners. I liked personality, but too much attitude turned me off, so I said no. I think he was surprised and probably not used to rejection. I was more interested in catching up with my friends whom I hadn't seen in months. Besides, I had been flirting with an old flame close by and my attention was diverted elsewhere.

But Eric, as I'd come to find was his name, was awfully cute – and persistent. He sent me a drink and came back again. He begged (haha, he really did!), "Come on, dance with me!" Again, I said no but he had effectively gained my full attention, and I was in the mood for romance. I could feel his stare no matter what direction I stood. He'd strategically placed himself in my line of sight. I would turn away and feel his gaze burn the back of my head. Over and over, there he was, moving to lock eyes again and smile at me from across the room with piercing blue eyes and his 6'2" manly man frame. I had never been pursued this intensely. He had a powerful presence. The attraction between us was palpable. I felt like an invisible thread was being weaved around me. I was hypnotized by his gaze and fighting the connection. My girlfriend Nathalie was intrigued by the mysterious stranger and asked, "Do you know him?" "I have no idea who he is." I replied. And in these parts, where everybody knew everyone, so that didn't happen often.

The next thing I knew, the live music was over, and the jukebox started playing as people left the dance floor and settled down between sets. My ears were still buzzing from the loud noise. The temporary reprieve was a nice break, and a way to make good use of this time to talk up a storm with my high school best friend. I felt a tap on my shoulder, paused mid-sentence, and turned to see who it was.

BAM! A set of lips landed on mine. Soft, gentle, eager, and promising.

What were his lips doing on my mouth? Well, wow, that had never happened to me before!

He was a very handsome man, and despite being strangers we felt something powerful. That kiss – my God! – it had fireworks in it. You know, the type of kiss where, in a romantic movie the girl slowly tiptoes and lifts one of her legs? WOW.

At that moment, lightning struck and set me on fire. I was left spellbound by a coup de foudre that would rock my world and carry me 20,000 nautical miles to the sea.

This is how I met my husband in 1989. He was a determined, self-assured, irresistible man and he didn't care what he had to do to get what he wanted.

In his life, it never dawned on him that he could fail or not accomplish what he set out to do. He pushes the boundaries beyond what anyone I knew was capable of, and frankly that has scared a few people in our orbit in the process. It has both inspired me, and driven me nuts!

My pool of possibilities was smaller then. I had barely left the shallow water and thought I had found freedom. Boy, was I wrong. Apparently, there was a vast ocean awaiting.

I grew up in a small, landlocked town with 12,500 residents. Cowansville, Québec is located about 250 miles away from the nearest ocean. I was a curious child with an artistic streak and a taste for the wild. Mom and Dad had their hands full with me always testing the boundaries of a very typical small-town life. As a teenager, I tested all the things—remember that movie *Dazed and Confused*—that was me. I smoked pot, skipped school, snuck out my bedroom window at night, and threw parties when my parents were away. I was also a good kid who did well in school, but just went a bit nuts when my hormones kicked in. I walked a swerving line between my wild streak and obeying the rules of my parent's house. I craved adventures and could not wait to leave for college. I dreamed of escaping to the big city and exploring the world.

When I met Eric, I thought I had made it. Doing the 9 to 5 in a fancy advertising firm, I had the freedom to do what I wanted. I loved the hustling and bustling of the metropolis, its high rises, nightlife, club scene, and discovering a world where everything did not walk a path of conformity.

I pushed the boundaries, but just enough to thrill me and yet remain within society's tolerable rebellion. Sometimes I went a bit overboard (no pun intended) while exploring the many possibilities presented to a daring young woman barely free of adult supervision.

When I look back at the woman-child I was, I thank my inquisitive nature and despite the times that it got me in trouble, I always found a way to safely get out of dicey situations and learn valuable lessons. You could say that I had the heart of an adventurer, but my small-town upbringing hadn't prepared me for the unconventional possibilities that would soon lift me off my feet.

The whirlwind romance between Eric and I opened my eyes to the big, wide world. There was SO MUCH more than the closest big city, breaking rules, and nonconforming – there were countries, lifestyles, cultures, and the whole world to explore!

While mine was a textbook rebellion, Eric was a profound seeker for what made him feel truly alive. A true wanderlust.

Embarking with him on our 20-year journey aboard Windsong was the natural progression of our free-spirited lives.* We were soul-searching, looking for solace by ways of expansion and freedom. Just two hippie bums trying to navigate life and our relationship, and willing to go the extra mile for one another.

It takes special chemistry between two individuals to live two decades in the same 41 x 13 foot space. We functioned within an eight foot radius, without killing each other. I'll admit to you that I may have simmered the thought of having him walk the plank once or twice! Ha!

What Windsong offered was possibilities. The possibilities of discovery, adventures, travel, growth, freedom, happiness, and wonder. And the possibility of sailing away from the bad influences that were creating havoc in our lives (or so I thought). We weathered experiences that allowed us to get to know ourselves under pressure, push our boundaries, explore the unknowns (internal and external), discover our strengths, survive immense challenges, and grow even closer through it all.

We were two kids who were searching for an expression of liberty larger than we could envision, the opportunity to reimagine our lives and break the mold that society was trying to squeeze us into. We cut the lines and ran away from what felt suffocating. We gave ourselves a fresh start where we could breathe wide and deep and go as far as our imagination could carry us.

We were different from the start and joining the 'liveaboard community' felt natural. Theirs was a welcoming tribe of eccentrics, misfits, freedom seekers, and adventurers, who sailed life on the outskirts of typical society. They all embraced other possibilities for their lives and so did we.

Windsong gave us a way out and captivated us with the romantic ideas of sailing the vast oceans and becoming masters of our destiny. Well, we might not have sailed around the world, but we sure as heck weren't swimming in the kiddie pool anymore.

LESSON: Align with possibilities

Of all the things I dreamed of when I was growing up, living aboard a sailboat for 20 years definitely wasn't on the radar. I can count on one hand the times I saw the ocean before I moved to Florida. I had never set foot on a sailboat until this amazing man—who would later become my husband—and I bought our first sailboat, a 25-foot MacGregor, Wannabe, in 1996. I was 28.[*]

He played a big part in expanding my boundaries. It was his dream to move to Florida, trade in our Harley leathers for flip flops, and move onto a sailboat, but I shared his excitement and appetite for adventure.

He's never doubted his ability to get what he wanted. And his enthusiasm for jumping feet-first into the craziest adventures and figuring it out as we go has always impressed me. Some of the times, I confess, it annoyed me to no end. Especially since I prefer to contemplate and plan out changes before taking big plunges, like moving to another country or tossing our life into vast seawaters and growing human gills. But my husband? He is impulsive. He has always felt as if he would run out of time, and therefore would rather cut the lines, raise the sails full steam ahead, and just pray that the coast is clear. He also has an incredible amount of luck. Our friend, Lacruz, calls us fortunate for our ability to always fall back on our feet—no matter what the circumstances.

When you're willing to play outside your boundaries and embrace the unknown, a world of possibilities is unveiled.

Yes, I've experienced BIG emotions, lots of self-doubts, and a landscape of fears. Learning to sail the unknown isn't always easy. Some periods have tested my strength, some were excruciatingly painful and left me wounded and weary, even doubting my decisions. Leaving everyone and everything that's familiar behind to start a new life, whether in a new country or floating on water, is bound to create waves.

But the things I have seen, the journey I've been on, and the people I have met have inspired the heck* out of me. None of it would be a reality if I hadn't aligned and embraced the possibilities the pregnant unknown carries. That day, when I *literally* embraced possibilities, a door opened, and my future came in.

QUESTION: I'll never forget the amazing feeling of…

 ACTION: Rev up your power center

It takes more than knowing what you want. Pursuing your interests ardently and passionately takes willpower. You must take conscious actions to make it happen and stay the course when obstacles arise.

If there is something that you want, claim it.

If there is something that you need, get it.

If there is something bothering you, change it.

If there is something missing, search for it.

Improve your willpower, act, and create the life you desire.

The source of our confidence and willpower lives in our solar plexus or third chakra** which is located a couple of inches above our bellybutton. This chakra helps us stand in our power and energizes us to move toward our desires. An imbalance in the solar plexus can cause a lack of self-esteem, mistrust, insecurity, a strong inner critic, as well as various digestive issues. Add physical exercises to strengthen your core and help put your metabolism in motion, stoking the fires within. This newfound vitality will help you activate your physical, mental, and emotional energy to support your goals.

Some of my favorite ways to accomplish this are core-focused sun salutation yoga, abdominal workouts, and deep belly breathing exercises—completely exhaling all the breath and releasing stagnant energy from your belly.

*(See book 1)

**Chi is the lifeforce that sustains us and is all around us. Chakras—meaning wheels—are spinning vortices and important parts of the body's subtle energy system through which our energy flows. Each chakra supports specific body functions, endocrine system, mental, emotional, and all aspects of our lives. They are affected by stress, environmental toxins, illness, trauma, and emotions, which can either constrict the flow of energy or create hyperactivity. Keeping our Chakras balanced, aligned, and activated is essential for the proper flow of our lifeforce energy.

2. Divers Down—Fishing for Live Ones

Align your Survival Instinct

Our friend Jovin trying to catch dinner.

"Everyone deserves a spot on the life raft." —*Carole*

Diving lets you experience out-of-this-world sensations, where you enter a completely self-sufficient ecosystem that is foreign, and potentially dangerous to you. One rarely sees its captivating beauty from up close. The vastness of the space around you is mesmerizing, and its dangers are oh-so present. It's one thing to gear up in daylight and see what danger lurks ahead, and a whole other to dive into dark waters at night, in pursuit of thrill and the occasional dinner. But in the deep unknown, the predator might turn into prey.

6/7/98: First Mate's Log

In the early days of sailing Windsong, we were young and fearless and had a rowdy crew of thrill-seeking friends who lived life with the I-am-young-and-invincible-and-will-never-die mentality. Everyone loves a good adventure, but what makes a gripping story is the danger and fear you conquer, replaced with a renewed gratitude for life.

On one of our first overnight trips on the "big" boat, we decided to head down to Matheson Hammocks, south of Miami, on Biscayne Bay. We had never spent time in this area and were eager to explore every available anchorage south of Fort Lauderdale. Honestly, any destination would have been fine as long as we were casting off and heading out to strengthen our sea legs.

This was the first time we sailed Windsong with all our possessions onboard. We'd owned it since December and had spent some months recommissioning it, painting, sealing, cleaning, and preparing it for life onboard. We'd sailed it lots, of course, but this trip felt different, it wasn't just a big toy we owned anymore, since we had moved aboard full-time, this was our home. We were keenly aware that if we sunk it, it would go down with all our belongings, and we'd be homeless. We also had a new sense of pride and maturity, brought on by our deep respect for the ocean and how unforgiving the environment can be.

Our guest for the weekend was our young friend Jovin, an avid fisherman passionate about lures and fishing toys, and he was currently very frustrated at having come up empty on his promise of a free meal. We had sailed from Port Everglades, passed by the busy Port of Miami, and came in through the channel at Stiltsville, just south of Key Biscayne, where we admired the village of pastel-colored houses built on stilts, and only accessible by boat, with the million-dollar view of the Miami Skyline, the ocean, and Biscayne Bay.

We'd sailed until late afternoon to give him as much time as possible to catch dinner before deciding it was a bust. The 10-knot wind and our 4.5 to 5 knots headway hadn't been enough for us to make it to our destination before dark, so we had kicked up the motor in the Bay in search of an anchoring spot for the night. We found a cozy place close to Matheson Hammock and Eric switched to his other favorite hobby—chef duty.

Throughout dinner, our friend couldn't stop talking about fish. He had brought a crazy amount of fishing gear onboard for our 2-day weekend and his eyes lit up when he talked about angling. He could not be deterred; he was going to catch something.

So, it was no surprise when after dinner, despite the looming darkness, he decided to dive and try his new speargun to see if he would have better luck underwater. A speargun uses a large rubber band to launch a spear tethered to the gun that impales fish.

Jovin was a strong young man, all muscles, and tendons from years of working construction, and an experienced diver. But, he was unfamiliar with his new weapon and had limited night-diving experience. We were in a calm bay with some boats bobbing gently in the early evening and there wasn't much current in the anchorage. The water was calm and a cozy 80 degrees. We told him that it might be best to wait till the morning but there was no stopping him, and our attitude back then was more of a "live and let live" approach. Of course, that was before years on the boat taught us to manage our crew. Thankfully, we never lost anyone!

He got all his gear and worked his way to the back of the boat, down the ladder, and onto our small swimming platform. He was passionate about diving and jumped at any chance to use his dive gear. On came the fins, strapped on the back went the tank, and down went the mask as he splashed into the warm, dark Miami waters, distorting the shimmering reflection from the city lights that danced across a fluid mirror.

Eric and I were in our own happiness bubble. We felt grateful for the amazing day we'd just had, sailing without a glitch, slightly sunburned and windburned with full bellies, we looked at each other with a satisfied grin, loving the feel of bobbing away on our floating home. We felt partly relieved and partly blessed, knowing that there was no turning back now. We were hooked and officially liveaboard sailors. It felt strangely grownup and as if we were breaking the rules at the same time.

We kept a careful watch on our friend following his air bubbles at the surface as he swam around the boat. We had thrown the diver's down buoy behind the boat and tied it to a cleat, making him promise not to venture too far from Windsong unless he came back to get it. This bobbing buoy has a six-foot-high pole with a divers-down flag tied to the top. The internationally recognized symbol of a red rectangle with a white diagonal stripe warns everyone to steer clear of 50 feet of distance because there are people in the water. We had turned on all deck lights and watched the last of the red sky turn deep grey.

I don't think he was down very long, 15 minutes at the most before he surfaced screaming and waving his arm up with the spear. "FONTAINE! Argh!" Figuring he'd had success, we quickly jumped to our feet. We looked at the spear end, but no fish. He swam frantically splashing his way toward the back of the boat as if Jaws was after him. We rushed to the swim platform feeling his panic. He was spent. His face was ghostly white, eyes wild with fear. His adrenaline had brought him back to the boat, yet he struggled to climb out of the water. What he had caught was himself. He had spearheaded his own hand. He had pulled the spear out and dark blood was coming out of his cramped fist. Eric grabbed him by the tank and helped lift him out, sitting him on the small swim platform long enough to take off his mask and tank, then half-carried, and half-dragged him up the ladder and into the cockpit.

He was howling in pain and swearing like bloody hell. I ran to get the first aid kit and a bright lantern for the cockpit. The night had grown dark, and we couldn't see a damn thing. He was shivering despite the 80-degree water and blurted out his story as Eric tried to calm him down and covered him with a dry towel. He needed to take a look closer and assess the damage. Thank goodness my husband took his first aid course and had his share of experience patching himself and his buddies from many bloody escapades.

Jovin didn't like the sight of blood, so he looked away. I went to get the bottle of rum and handed it to my husband who took the cap off and placed it in our friend's good hand. "Take a swig, man, this is going to hurt." (Flashback to cowboy movies! Hee Haw!)

All Jovin could talk about was the large shark/shadow he thought he saw. In his panic, he tried to spear it but missed. When he tried to reload, the spear slid off and shot in his hand. If it had been a shark, the bloody hand would have been a definite indicator that dinner was served. Poor guy thought he wouldn't be able to make it back to the boat before being shark bait.

Eric had to decide if we needed to get our friend to shore and to a hospital. Jovin was complaining every time he looked at his hand, "Oh my God, I'm going to faint, look at all the blood." He had a slight blood phobia, mostly to his own, and felt dizzy, refusing to look at it again. The last thing we needed was for him to faint, so Fontaine went on doctor's duty. He grabbed Jovin's arm, turned his back to him, and immobilized it under his armpit so that the only thing our friend could see was Eric's back.

"Take a swig of Captain Morgan, buddy, Captain Fontaine is on the job." Perfectly appropriate as he sat on our Morgan 41' while our Captain checked his hand. (If you haven't read book #1 yet, Windsong is a Morgan OutIslander Ketch).

First, Eric assessed where the spear had entered. It ran through his hand between his index and middle finger, maybe ¾ of an inch down the palm. It made a clean hole through between the knuckles. Eric grabbed his wrist and asked him to move his fingers.

Despite the pain and the blood gushing out, they were all wiggling. He was a lucky man. Half an inch to the left or the right and he could have severed a nerve or a muscle and done serious damage to his hand for life. His five digits were intact, so we didn't have to make an emergency midnight dinghy trip to the shore, anchor with an injured deckhand in a place we didn't know, and figure out how to transport him to an ER.

Satisfied that only minor "surgery" would be needed, another large swig of rum was prescribed. Some to numb the pain and some to calm the nerves. We would have to rename our buddy JC after the bleeding hole in his hand. (Please forgive me Jesus—I can't help myself.)

Eric dug in and surveyed the damage more closely, as I assisted and held the spotlight. He disinfected the wound and bandaged him up really well. We offered to dinghy him to shore again, but he declined. All his fingers were moving so we gave him some pain medicine, and he crashed like a log, his adrenaline spent and exhausted from his fright.

Eric and I looked at each other shaking our heads. Boys and their toys, trouble always soon follows. With peace restored, we retired for our needed sleep.

There's nothing like the feeling of waking up at anchor even when it's overcast. The sound of the water against the hull and the bobbing at the end of an anchor chain make my heart happy. JC was already up enjoying his first overnight stay on Windsong. He slept well he said, despite waking up once from his throbbing hand, he was content.

We took a peek at his hand and changed his bloodied bandage for fresh gauze. It looked good considering the trauma, and despite the swelling, all his fingers still functioned so he assured us that he didn't need to run to shore to spend the morning at a doctor's office. He preferred to stay onboard and fish for one more day. Jovin was clearly obsessed with fishing. I can't say that I understand it, but I respect his passion. He was a tough guy, bless his soul, he'd wait to see the doctor until he was home, proclaiming, "I have some fish to catch!"

Off we went, leaving our anchorage and waving goodbye to the invisible shark—silently thanking him for not having devoured our friend as human sushi. We turned our gaze to the east, raised the sails and off we went! We crossed Biscayne Bay and sailed out to sea the same way we came, carefully avoiding the surrounding sand flats near the iconic houses, following the channel to clear the coastal shallows. We charted a northern course a few miles from shore and aimed Windsong's bow toward Fort Lauderdale.

Chapter 2 — Align your Survival Instinct

The seas were rougher that day, and we were surrounded by grey skies, sailing between clouds, and staying dry. It was a dreary Monday morning so there was barely anyone out on the water except for the occasional daring fishermen on the horizon. We had the entire playground to ourselves.

Our one-handed fisherman was trying to catch fish while we sailed, which is quite a feat to do in between all the stays and running lines on a sailboat, let alone doing it with a gauze mitten on one extremity. He had brought so many lures onboard that I think he scared the fish.

We were about four to five miles offshore, sailed past the port of Miami on our port (left) side, and plowed through the waves. Windsong was under full sails. It's a 'ketch' so, there are two masts and with the genoa, main, and mizzen sails up, we skated over the water. It was a beautiful sight, and we were barely getting salty. The wind was starting to kick up at 23 knots, and our GPS said we were doing a good 8.8 knots over ground, since we were in the Gulf Stream our ride was maybe an actual 6 knots which was a decent sail.

(1 knot = 1 nautical mile per hour = 1.15 mph on land (1.85 km/h).

We passed an anchored 20-foot skiff far to our port side, between us and the Miami shores, and saw a diver's down flag. Steering clear of them we pushed on and made sure we detoured far and wide, still shredding our personal sailing speed record and writing it down for the books.

A mile later, Eric's eagle eyes spotted movement far to our starboard side out further offshore. Out of curiosity, we made a slight course adjustment to sail by and investigate. You never know what you might find floating out there. As we got closer, we realized that we could see an arm waving desperately for help. We were coming up fast and saw two men treading water, trying to catch our attention. We figured they had to be the divers from the boat we'd seen earlier. Miles from shore and incapable of swimming back to the safety of their boat, they were caught in a dangerous chop that was carrying them out to an angry sea. Without a soul in sight, we were their only chance.

We were under full sails and coming in at ramming speed. A boat like ours under full sails doesn't stop on a dime to pick up stationary men overboard, especially in choppy and windy conditions. The quickest way for us to get them to safety was to circle around, slow our speed down, and get a line close enough for them to grab and hold on to on our second pass. We had a man-overboard rescue buoy in the shape of a "U" which we tied to the end of a line and threw in the water, we veered the boat around and made a dangerous jibe* and took no time to adjust the sails, which flopped angrily at the sudden change of direction—they could take the abuse—we were in a hurry to get these gentlemen to safety.

> * You *jibe* when you turn the stern (back) of the boat through the wind. This maneuver is not recommended in strong winds as it forcefully and quickly moves your boom, and sails to the other side, exerting much force on the hardware and canvas and a potential danger to inattentive crew. You may be more familiar with the sailing term tacking which is the opposite when you turn the bow (front) of the boat through the wind.

The motor had overheated earlier that day after we pushed it a little too hard forging our way into an impromptu boat race with a "friendly" that was sailing out of the inlet. The engine had not cooled down enough for us to restart it. So, we quickly made a plan of action for a sailing rescue.

As we came about the divers, we saw that both men had discarded their dive tanks, the unnecessary weight added to the difficulty of staying afloat, and they were probably empty and useless by now. One of them was actually carrying a spear gun. The irony.

We slowed down as much as we could in the gusty wind while trying to maintain our direction. The lesser the speed, the harder it is to maneuver a sailboat. We sailed by them close enough so that the line and buoy floated right by the men who caught it. We caught two fish!! Who says fishing ain't fun?! What a surreal moment of absolute ecstasy for these two exhausted men. The adrenaline was quite high on Windsong as well.

Now, we could have continued to gradually slow our speed, bring the three sails down, stop to bring the men on board, and then motor them to their boat. But the men were armed. In distress, but armed and at sea.

If there is one thing that my captain doesn't trust, it's strangers with a weapon. No matter what the situation.

We were still making way having just slowed down enough to grab them and had them in tow. "Are you all right?" We screamed. Thumbs up and huge grins, all we could see was the white of their teeth smiling. "Is that your boat?" pointing to the direction of the abandoned skiff we had passed shortly before. "Yes!" They pointed to their boat with a thumbs up, looking ecstatic with relief. The men were unhurt. The older diver looked completely wiped but his younger mate was strong and had him in a bear grip inside the horseshoe float. We wouldn't let them escape; they were safe.

Through sign language and huge grins, they waved us on toward their boat.

This was, after all, Miami waters, home of Miami Vice for a reason. We know of stories that would raise the hair on the back of your neck so we were relieved when they motioned us to keep going. Stopping would not have been a problem but it was much easier and faster to simply tow them a few minutes and drop them off at their skiff.

We continued to luff the sails and slow down to make their ride as comfortable as possible. We kept a watchful eye on them and reached their boat, making a sort of half circle, avoiding collision then veering in front of the skiff so that the line with our passengers would steer directly onto their vessel. Our divers had let go of our buoy and successfully landed beside their swim platform.

By then, we had finally slowed down and gone downwind in 3 to 5-foot seas. It would have taken us this long to extract them from the water. We slowly turned back and circled their boat, adjusting sails as we passed and not wanting to leave until we knew they were okay.

The younger man was climbing onto their swimming platform, his friend still in the water, just holding on to the safety of their boat. They both looked exhausted, especially the older man treading water. I'm not sure how long he would have lasted out there. He didn't have the energy to lift himself out of the water just yet and was probably thanking his good fortune for having come this close. I'm sure they were both conscious of how tragically close to death they had come. His buddy thanked us and signaled that all was okay as he reached for his friend. We wished them well and waved goodbye to two very lucky individuals who probably kissed the ground the moment they docked.

Diving is an amazing sport that will make you travel into a world beyond your imagination. But every environment has its dangers. Awareness is key to staying safe. We were very grateful that we had been in the right place and at the right time to save the day. Thanks to Eric's keen sense of observation, two divers would be going home to their families with a tale to tell. And another diver would learn a great lesson in awareness, get to keep his hand, and fish another day.

A hole in one hand and a miracle at sea. I can't say if JC was involved, but I sure am glad for how fortunate we all were that weekend.

PS Jovin got his hand checked out when we came to shore, and the doctor told him that whoever fixed his wound did an excellent job and that nothing else needed to be done except to prescribe a round of preventative antibiotics. First aid knowledge would come in handy through the years on Windsong!

LESSON: Align your survival instinct

I have faced death many times in my life. It's a simple fact. The more adventures you go on, the more trouble you're bound to get into. (And the more fun you're going to have!) Every time I faced danger or feared physical harm, I've felt my instincts take over until I was out of harm's way—only to later collapse and ask myself, "How did I make it through that?"

Our natural survival instinct is a genetically hard-wired, innate force that lives within all beings prompting a furious fight when threatened by danger.

Whether we face a life and death situation or *THINK* we do, our sympathetic nervous system activates and kicks our body and mind into overdrive, flooding our bodies with stress hormones like adrenaline and cortisol which create instant physical and psychological changes to prepare us to take self-preservation measures and get away from danger.

The fear our friend Jovin felt seeing a shadow and thinking that it was a predator coming to eat him felt the same to him as if he had actually seen a shark. The fear our stranded divers felt envisioning their disappearance and drowning at sea flooded their bodies with enough adrenaline to wade and stay afloat despite being undeniably exhausted. Once people reach safety, they often collapse with no energy left to move a finger.

There's been many times when I have felt post-danger exhaustion and the post-adrenaline crash that follows these experiences. Fortunately, as the shock wears off, an infusion of exhilaration for being alive, gratitude for breaths, the need to hug your loved ones, the absolute resolve to live your best darn life every single day, and maybe even a kiss on the ground when you 'reach the shore' all start to swirl inside.

It's normal and essential to have those reactions in the middle of an ocean when we think we're going to die. Unfortunately, modern-life stresses have become high enough to activate people's survival instincts with a simple bad day at the office, or a traffic jam. Our stress hormones have become consistently on high alert and get depleted, zapping our energy.

They can also be triggered by feelings of insecurity from losing our homes, jobs, or facing health issues. Our sense of security is governed by our first chakra located at the tip of the tailbone. This chakra helps us ground ourselves to feel more rooted in stability and safety.

The biggest danger in letting our insecurities and stresses run wild is that we may not be able to discern when true danger arises and act when needed or we may shush the inner voice that's trying to help us when we should act.

People often fall victim to scams or bad actors when their instincts have been screaming 5-star alarms. Pay attention, listen, and learn to recognize when your instincts are on the dot or inaccurate. Nurture that connection so that it thrives and becomes more dominant.

I've often felt ungrounded on the boat as we faced dangers from storms, hurricanes, sinking, getting hurt, or lost. An instability brought on by the failure to provide basic needs—food, water, shelter, safety, or emotional connection—triggers our survival instincts to shift our priorities and make sure that we are safe and secure.

When we are not in a dire situation, a practice of becoming aware of when our stress is triggered is a very beneficial first step in releasing it so that we can then relax and again become present, rooted in our bodies.

Chapter 2 — Align your Survival Instinct

I realign myself by acknowledging that I feel stress, then assess if my stress is valid, then take appropriate actions to resolve my insecurities.

These days I have a saying, whether we're on land or water, "If we're not going to sink, don't sweat it."

QUESTION: I am insecure (about/when)…

 ACTION: Superhero pose
When feeling insecure or facing a sudden stressful situation, do the Superhero Pose to project and disperse anxious energy. (This is also great for strengthening your third chakra.)

- Stand with fists on hips

Straighten and lengthen your back

- Push shoulders down and back to open your heart/chest
- Pull navel (bellybutton) in and up
- Ground feet into the floor
- Look straight ahead
- Imagine that you are drawing in energy from the earth through the soles of your feet and bringing it up through your legs all the way up to your heart
- Truly feel the presence, weight, and support Mother Earth gives you
- Visualize bringing energy down from the sun through the top of your head, all the way to your heart where it blends with the earth's energy and charges you up like a solar-powered battery
- Breath deeply in and out, and smile

- Hold the pose for at least 3 minutes and do it as often as you need, before meetings, or when you feel insecure or nervous.
- Whatever you're doing today, do it with the confidence of a 4-year-old in a Batman t-shirt. You've got this!

3. James Bond's Cave—On a Mission to Glee

Align your Actions with Joy

Carole and her dad, André, at the entrance of Thunderball.

"Joy is the current in a sea of possibilities" —Carole

The Mission: Give my Canadian parents—big-time landlubbers, aka land people—the time of their lives on our floating home far away from anything they have ever known, in a tropical country they have never visited.

Pickup Point: Nassau, Bahamas

Destination: The Exumas

Objective: Sparkle their life with fantastic adventures, wild encounters, and bedazzle them with such excitement and enthusiasm for our lifestyle that they understand how their only daughter moved thousands of miles away to float on a boat with a big and loud Viking man-child.

June of 2008,

We had tried to bring my parents to the Bahamas the previous year, but bad weather and choppy seas had sunk our plans. Crossing the Gulf Stream from Fort Lauderdale to The Bahamas is just a day trip, but timing is essential, and conditions can turn quickly. You can expect anything from one extreme to the other. The typical seven hour crossing can turn into a never-ending day of beating the seas, the elements, and your head for departing in such weather. Or, the day brings zero wind, a flat ocean that reflects back your boredom, and lulled sails that inspire prayers to Aeolus (aka Njǫrd, God of the Wind). "May we have at least a puff of breeze to scootch us forward," is chanted while scanning the horizon hoping to see anything of interest. The aim is to cross somewhere in the middle.

Knowing that this could be the scariest part of the trip for my parents, we opted to fly them directly from Canada to The Bahamas, and sail 87 miles to New Providence Island to pick them up in Nassau.

We knew the four of us got along great in tight quarters because we had taken them on a few overnight trips. We had always stayed close to shore in South Florida, but his time we were going full-on tropical with them.

We have great synergy and always have a good time vacationing together. You can love your friends and family, but it doesn't mean that you all want to be within 10 feet of each other for 10 days. Lucky for us, Mom and Dad are great company. They have been married for 59 years and are devoted to each other. It's a beautiful relationship.

Still, days sailing the islands aren't the same as an overnighter close to Miami. The prospect of having them on board for two weeks made me a little nervous. The unavoidable unknowns and 41 feet of space could test our lovey-dovey togetherness. I wanted everything to be perfect and as we know, perfection is rarely achieved - let alone in a fluctuating environment at the mercy of the elements, where the next wave can bring about the adventure of a lifetime.

So, after Eric and I talked, we sent them an invitation. My parents are 100% landlubbers with no desire to grow gills. My dad is adventurous but never traveled by boat. Neither has Mom, who is a bit nervous around the water. Nevertheless, they said "YES!" and booked their exotic getaway. This was going to be memorable.

Chapter 3 — Align your Actions with Joy

It had been a bit of a rough passage for Eric and me with churning seas that slowed down our progress, and we had barely made it in time after sailing non-stop for the last three days. We had made the right decision to fly them directly there. We showed up a little raggedy looking but in time to see their faces come out of the cab and walk down the marina docks with luggage in tow. Dad had on his Hawaiian vacation shirt and straw hat, and Mom was wearing the biggest relief-at-seeing-us grin, sandals, and snazzy beige Bermuda shorts. They were so far out of their element—with butterflies fluttering on their insides—they appeared happy as clams to see that their daughter and her man-child-Viking had made it to our rallying point.

To let their bodies acclimate to the motion of the boat, we decided to stay there overnight and just explore Nassau. It's always best to let your landlubbing guests spend 24 hours sleeping onboard before departure. This eases seasickness and when in port we have a/c to help the transition into tropical heat.

We did the obligatory dinghy ride to Paradise Island, visited the luxurious resort, walked the white sandy beaches, dipped our toes in the clearest tropical water, explored the man-made lagoons, and viewed their impressive story-high aquariums. This is one of the 10 largest in the world—filled with eight million gallons of ocean water and giant fish, dolphins, rays, sharks, and every imaginable sea creature. After the shocking $15 rums in Atlantis, we told them that this was the last of luxury they would see on this trip. We had plenty of cheap rum onboard and would sail away at first light.

We spent the next weeks creating precious memories with our explorer hats on, binoculars in hand, sailing with dolphins, swimming to exotic beaches, hand-feeding birds, inspecting whale bones, star gazing, and visiting many uninhabited islands—each offering their own treasures of marvel.

But the day that will forever be engraved in my father's heart was diving into the James Bond cave.

At approximately 24.1703 degrees north, and 76.4404 degrees west, there is a raggedy-looking low-lying island bordering the entrance channel to Staniel Cay. This is a highly sought-after destination for cruisers exploring the outskirts of the Exumas, known for its quiet remoteness, pristine waters, and friendly islanders.

With only Cat Island between it and 7,777 miles of open waters to the coast of Africa, the ocean here exploded with sea life. The Exuma Sound delineated a drastic rise on the sea floor and it gifted us with a line of beautiful islands to explore. Back then, there were almost no tourists in sight except for a few private vessels. The pace of island life is languorously slow as if the hourglass spins a pearl on the dripping sand of time. Everywhere you go there is minimal action expected through the heat of day, and everyone seems to be in a permanent good mood.

We arrived the day before and anchored less than a mile away in a shallow area by the northwest side of Staniel.

To a passerby, it looked like a deserted mound of sharp coral land, just large enough for some shrubbery and a few bird's nests. But to the adventurous spirit who is willing to dive under and look within, it blesses you with its hidden treasure.

The Thunderball Grotto is one of the most breathtaking spots in the world and the most beautiful natural wonders I have seen in my life, so far. Surrounded by pristine waters, the cave is strategically placed in a road-less-traveled area of the Exumas. The sea life in and around it is awe-inspiring. It gets its name from the 1965 James Bond movie *Thunderball* where it was featured. So impressive that it's been filmed in many Hollywood movies including another James Bond, *Splash*, and Jessica Alba's *Into the Blue*. The only reason why it remains pristine to this day, despite its fame, is its remote location far from any populated area where most traffic is local Bahamian or sailors exploring the outskirts and lesser-known islands in the Exumas, and that it can only be accessed by boat. Plus, one has to know that there is such a cave hidden underneath this pile of rock. It's an X on the map if you know where to look.

We planned our outing with the low slack tide. Slack tide is the brief period of time when the water isn't going up or down and is otherwise calm and without tidal current. It happens right before the tide reverses up or down. Choosing slack low tide meant that there would be more of the cave out of the water, and we would minimize the current we would have to swim through.

There are multiple underwater entrances for divers, but to make it easy on Dad, we waited for low tide to simply snorkel into one of the two accessible entrances at low water and avoid the strong currents. Mom, not being a big swimmer, opted to wait for us in the dinghy and enjoy the sun while we went on our James Bond mission. We equipped Dad with a mask, snorkel, noodle, and fins before leaving so he was geared up and ready to go. Dad was raised on a farm and had always been a landlubber, so this was WAY outside of his comfort zone. He was a bit anxious but super-psyched about going into the deep blue to dive into a cave with us (how brave!). It was extremely hot and sunny that day and we welcomed the water adventure. We motored our dinghy around the tiny island to the other side of the single navigable channel to the island and chose a spot where there would be less wake from boat traffic. Even if this was a calm place, just one bad wake could be scary and unpleasant to swim in for a novice. We anchored our dinghy in about 11 feet of water, right behind the island.

My heart was thrilled, and I could feel my excitement build up because I knew what was about to happen. It had been a year since our last visit, and I could not wait to share this adventure with Dad. He looked nervous and excited. It was funny to see my dad in snorkeling gear in a dinghy in the Bahamas. I would have never imagined this in my wildest dreams, yet here we were.

There were a few other boats and a handful of divers around. We geared on, squeezed a few drops of baby shampoo in our mask as a defogger, and jumped in the cool sapphire water. For my dad who swam in a pool most of his life, just swimming in 11 feet of open ocean surrounded by larger fish was an adventure. But the mission had just started. Eric and I exchanged excited glances and surrounded him front and back while he put his snorkel on and tested how to breathe underwater. We adjusted his mask and fins, and waited until he got his bearings and felt comfortable in his apparatus to swim away. We waved goodbye to Mom—whose joy was to relax in the bobbing sun—and kicked our fins toward the island.

At first, the only thing we could see was the mound of dried-up brush. But then at water level, an entrance opened, swallowing the sea and everything around it, like you were swimming into a whale's mouth, and everything disappeared in the darkness. As our eyes adjusted, we swam on with Eric leading the way, Dad in the middle, and I closed the ranks. We swam in a tighter space, like entering an underwater tunnel, feeling rocks and island on each side, kicking our fins and following shadows and shapes, we used our hands to guide us and protect us from bumping into the rocks, we veered to the right and felt the space around us expand. We knew we made it inside. We came up for air, and the sight took our breath away. "WOW!" we shouted in unison! Despite the stronger current outside, it was like a pool on the inside of the cavern. We were in the belly of the island, which was completely hollowed out, and even had gaping holes on top, creating natural skylights allowing sun rays to pierce through, and create amazingly stunning light effects all around us. In certain places, the ceiling was 20 feet high, but in others, you had to watch your head coming up or risk breaking skin from the sharpness of the coral. The sun's rays made the water glimmer like diamonds and bounced light off the most adorable colorful fish that were filling the cave, competing with us for a space to swim.

Through one of the lower openings, you could see the neighboring island and felt like you were in a submerged submarine peering out.

I imagined pirates hiding treasures here hundreds of years ago. What a sacred space. Sounds bounced off the eroded wall, echoing along the splashing water, our voices muffled yet louder as if in a speaker. No matter, no words could express what we were witnessing except a flabbergasted, "WOW!"

Dad could now view firsthand the stunning beauty around him. His anxiety was gone, replaced by exhilaration and immense gratitude. This was the best mission ever. He relaxed, and we let ourselves be smitten by this new world. We were surrounded by a mecca of gentle wildlife. Fish painted the kaleidoscope water, their scales reflecting the sun's rays like prisms. We swam alongside yellow-tail snappers with their fluorescent tails and skinny bodies that were quick to race out of the way, and the less obvious spotted striped groupers with their forever disapproving frowned faces, red squirrel fish that looked like they had a black eye, and hundreds of little sergeant majors all on standby waiting for orders in their black stripes and yellow uniforms swimming sharp turns with their assertive attitudes.

The parrot fish were larger than I'd ever seen, nibbling on coral with their pursed lips and sharp teeth. Many less obvious species crowded the tunnel system, some large enough to feed a family. The lobsters loving the protective environment had created a maze of hiding places and were scrambling in and out of every hole.

My favorites were the angelfish with their elegant flowing fins of different shapes and colors and ethereal appearance. Those are the ones often seen in fancy tropical aquariums—except here they were four times the size! They looked like they were painted by a grand master with the most striking color combinations; cobalt blues alternating with sunshine yellows and glowing lilacs. The colors overflowed and dripped onto the many coral fish in the cave all gathered in the illuminated center like a dance floor—turn on some good island music like Eric Stone singing *Humuhumunukunukuapua* (Hawaiian fish "so colorful that he glows") and we had ourselves a bonafide reef party!

It was an extraordinary gift to not only see their natural habitat but to swim in it. I had the overwhelming feeling of floating out in space, being reincarnated as a mermaid, breathing into Jacques Cousteau's snorkel, and stepping into Aladdin's treasured cavern. Every cell in my body screamed, "Happiness! Joy! Joy!" I was floating on cloud nine. Oh wait, I WAS floating…in paradise!!

We explored every nook and cranny fascinated by curious creatures knocking on our masks, or nonchalant old timers looking grumpy as they swam past our fins. The sunlight made them sparkle and created beams like an underwater light show. We admired the brilliantly colored reefs and swam to other entrances and saw multiple openings beneath the waves. The rock formation was so much fun to discover. All three of us got lost in our exploration, dreaming, admiring details, and appreciating the peace of aquatic life.

We made our way out and bobbed to the surface. We were all wearing perpetual grins. What a magnificent sight! The greatest gift was witnessing my dad's boyhood delight. I feel freaking blessed to have been able to give him this experience. The emotions in his eyes said it all; he was bedazzled. Awestruck, he simply asked, "Can we go back?" adding, "I wish Mom was here to see this."

Of course, we obliged and said, "We can stay as long as you want," as we adjusted our masks and swam back in.

Suddenly, we felt a commotion and the space inside the cave was frenzied with action.

"Whoa, what is going on?!" We wondered.

A woman had just entered the cave and was rummaging with a large bag. She finally got it opened and within seconds was surrounded by a sea of tropical fish. She was hand-feeding them!

The food disappeared as fast as it came out and she turned to make her way into the tunnel and out of the cave. A cloud of bubbles and fish followed suit and so did we.

As soon as she came out in the open and left the cavern, she was engulfed in a swarm of tropical fish. Like a fast-moving underwater river gushing over her offerings, the fish cloud engulfed her and her whole upper body disappeared and all we could see was her finned feet kicking and swimming to stay in place. She became a moving mass of tropical fish. It was hilarious and astonishing. She wasn't in any danger, but they gobbled up her treats faster than she could get them out. Hundreds of them, of all colors of the rainbow, all fighting to get their share, and all moving in a somewhat unison current like a bird flock in the sky. It was absolutely fascinating.

Talk about a change of perspective from feeding tiny fish in a tank, to being inside the tank where fish ten times bigger were being fed in this natural habitat.

And just like that, they were gone. The food disappeared and they were on to the hunt. She was grinning from ear to ear, and we all gave her a big thumbs-up.

We surfaced to talk. A few dinghies were arriving so the place would get a bit more crowded. Eric had had enough and decided to go back to the dinghy and join Mom. I looked at Dad and his enthusiasm was contagious, so we went in for the third time. I let Dad take the lead now that he knew his way around. Swimmers were entering the cave and he was good on his own, so I left him to explore the other side of a maze and made my way to the east side of the island. It was so cool to swim through these pathways, and gently flow through the abundant sea life. The last time I had been there I had seen a large shark in the distance looking toward Staniel Cay, but lucky for us, none were spotted that day! We saw a gentle turtle slowly making its way into the depths of the bay.

We burned every detail to memory, framed pictures in our minds, and interacted with every fish we encountered, waving goodbye to them, and thanking the Thunderball Grotto for blessing us with its inner sanctum; its mystical belly.

Dad told us that he was amazingly proud of himself despite having been nervous in the beginning. Deep down the little boy in him had been very excited to make a big splash. He felt immensely rewarded with all that he had seen, and his heart was bursting with joy. If you had told him just days earlier at the Atlantis Aquarium that instead of being an outsider with his nose glued to the glass, marveling at the mysterious underwater world, he would be gallivanting in nature's 352 quintillion gallon ocean, swimming with beautiful creatures, and interacting with the abundant sea life—he certainly would not have believed you.

To this day, it's my dad's favorite adventure onboard Windsong. His eyes light up when he tells the story of the time he swam into a National Geographic documentary.

Dad, you truly are a 007 for having done so.

LESSON: Align your actions with joy

Whether or not you decide to pursue something—let your actions be aligned with joy. Dad felt adventurous and was rewarded with quite a tale. Mom felt like kicking her feet up and enjoying the tropical sun, and enjoyed her soul-filling quiet time.

I never want guests to do things they don't want to out of obligations or expectations. Actions should be taken out of joy. Joy is the compass rose, the destination, and the reason why we do most things. The more we tap into how joy feels inside our bodies, the more in tune with spirit, secure in ourselves, confident in our choices, strong in our voice, at peace with our environment, and aligned in our chakras we will be.

This flowing activated energy will guide you toward living a healthier, happier life. Let joy be your North Star.

QUESTION: In what ways can I be more adventurous?

 ACTION: Dive buddy

Collaborations and partnerships help us reach our goals. Engage a friend as your "dive buddy" to sail to your goal. It must be a supportive and reliable person in your life. Declare what you want out loud and ask them to check in on you, hold you accountable, and be honest when you slack off. Offer the same support to them so the relationship is synergetic, becoming accountability partners. This will help you keep your commitment and lend you courage when you need it. If you can't find anyone, hire a coach. This can make a difference between a dream staying a dream, or a checkmark on your bucket list!

4. A Shitty Day—Kills the Mood

Align with Authenticity

> *"Positivity can be toxic if it comes at the cost of authenticity."* —Carole

We all have chores we'd rather avoid at all costs. For my husband it's plumbing, for me, it's the laundromat. I've been onboard 20 years and there's no room for a washer and dryer on a 41' Morgan. That means that I've been shoveling dirty clothes for around 20 years, from one laundromat to another. Some of the places I've been to were dicey, and I've almost gotten beat up once by a scary ghetto woman who was high on something, and adamant about screaming at me while accusing me of stealing her washer in a sea of empty machines. Hate is a strong word, but I highly dislike going to laundromats.

Eric would rather do anything else on earth than work with drains and sanitation systems. We've had a drip under the galley sink for years. He tried to fix it when we bought the boat, but it continued to leak. A tiny annoying one-drop drip. Over a decade, he tried seals, flex tape, sealants, and replacement parts, and it's still leaking. It's a running joke—about the running leak. It's not like there aren't any leaks on board, there is ALWAYS a leak somewhere on older boats. But usually, leaks come from outside.

If there is one thing I have to say about my husband, it's that he can fix anything on board... when he wants to. If I complain and plead with him to fix something, he jokingly says, "You don't need to remind me every six months, I told you I would do it!"

On one of our many sailing excursions, we had been sailing north from Miami and heeling hard to port (left) all day. The direction of the waves slammed us to portside and made the hull bang hard on the water for the better part of four hours. It wasn't the most comfortable ride, but it was a gorgeous day, and you know what they say, "Any day out on the water is better than a day at the office!"

I was enjoying the gorgeous sun and tanning my buns when a whiff of stink grabbed my nose. You rarely smell bad odors out on the ocean. I went down below to investigate. SHIT! It was us that stank. I walked toward the bow room, and my nostrils shrieked. Peeeeeeyew! I gagged and ran upstairs as fast as I could. "Honey! It smells like poo in the bow room!"

I grabbed the helm while he went searching for the source of the awful smell. Yup, it definitely smelled like feces, but he couldn't see anything obvious in the bathroom, and the head (marine toilet) seemed fine. He raised the bed cushions and the stench increased. The toilet's holding tank lived in a stowage compartment in the bow room. The bladder had burst and the contents were splashing loose in the quartered section under the bed. This space was irregular, so the previous owners had installed a flexible bladder instead of a hard holding tank. You pay for it in durability. And since a boat is always on the move, things like this rub, eventually chafe, and give way. Today was the day the bow room holding tank decided to explode.

It was literally a shitty situation.

We could not avoid taking care of right away. Don't forget, we lived aboard and were sleeping inside that night. The sewage smell was so bad that I couldn't stay below. I'd throw up today's lunch, and tomorrow's for that matter.

Chapter 4 — Align with Authenticity

To make it worse, it was over 90 degrees and very humid. Eric would have to spend the next hour in a sweaty stinky shitty mess. God bless this man!

We would have to somehow secure the boat so he could get a grip on it. Luckily, we were sailing by a mooring field near Dania Beach, so we decided to pick up a mooring ball.

A mooring buoy is permanently anchored to the bottom of the ocean floor. Boaters can securely tie to it. The trick is to slow down as much as possible, letting the bow (front) of your boat come as close as possible so that an extended boat hook can grab the buoy line that can be tied to the front of the vessel. It's more challenging than it sounds. The closer the buoy, the more the boat hull hides it and the captain can't see from the wheel where to align the boat with the buoy. Picture little 'ole me, holding a 12 foot boat hook out with my arms at maximum extension, stretched over the stanchions on the bow, while trying to stay ON the boat. I held on with my legs while my body and one hand held the pole and the other hand gestured with my audible directions, "Left! Right! Slow down! The other way! Reverse!"

It wouldn't be so difficult if we didn't have to do this floating on water at the mercy of waves, wind, and currents. As I explained earlier, the slower a boat moves in the water, the less control you have over its direction, and the more the ocean takes control over you. This makes any slow ride in waves bumpy.

The bow is the worst place to be if you're motion-sensitive. Grabbing a mooring buoy is like trying to accomplish precision agility while being thrown in every direction. We'd rise on each wave, then slam down. Slapped by seawater, I'd gesture directions to my captain and try to hold on without slipping in wet conditions.

As I tried to grab the somewhat fixed floating target that floats and moves around with every wave, the pole flies left, right, up, and down along with the waves. The trick is to anticipate our movement and the direction of waves to create the perfect alignment. Oh, and this must be done without running over the buoy, otherwise, we'd have to sail past it, make a large circle to come back, and start the process over. Thankfully, we'd done it many times before, so I had a lot of practice and my aim was improving.

When at the helm, a captain can't hear people while they're facing forward screaming in the wind, so, hand signals are the way to go. With my death grip on my right hand, I reached out, pointing with my left arm for the captain to urgently turn left.

The bigger the waves, the rockier and wetter the ride. Wearing glasses and grippy shoes is highly recommended. I love it.

Honestly, I could have done this all day—since the bow of the boat was the only place where the air was fresh and pure that day! Ha!

I grabbed the mooring on the first try and tied our boat while the captain dove into the toxic pool.

Being moored allowed Windsong to put its nose in the wind (pun intended) and helped stabilize the boat, minimizing the rock'n rolling so Eric could contain the spill and clean up the mess.

There was still some splishing and splashing happening; such a shitty situation. I'm sorry Eric, but I could not help thinking it was funny! Of course—I wasn't the one elbows deep in caca.

I stayed on deck with a buddy of ours who had been fishing in the back of the boat. He thought the whole situation was hilarious too. Neither of us could suffer past the stinky fumes, so we went for a swim and some snorkeling.

Have I mentioned that my husband was my hero?!

Down below, the captain put his hands to work in a pile of steaming poo. First, he had to find and remove the hose clamps that would disconnect the hoses and remove the bladder. The problem was that sewage was sloshing everywhere and made everything slippery. How he didn't throw up amazes me. I would have been in the fecal, ahem, I mean fetal position (I couldn't resist). A lot of cursing ensued during the process, but the screwdriver finally found the clamps, and off came the hoses. The bladder was free to come out, if he could grab it! By his account, it was splishing and splashing and because of its rubbery material, every time he thought he had it, it would slip out of his hands with the next wave and slosh back into the crap. I couldn't stop laughing or exclaiming, "I'm sorry, babe!" The mess was overflowing and dripping everywhere, but he finally came got a grip on it (no gloves mind you), and made a beeline for the garbage bag.

We could smell the action from the top deck and hear his extreme indignation supported by colorful curse words flying out in steady steam. Out came the cleaning supplies and he scrubbed the mess away. The whole process took under an hour and the mess was finally contained. My hero! He truly saved the day. After disinfecting the locker, he jumped in the shower to disinfect the man—he stayed in there an awfully long time!

It was partly breathable again in our home. We would have to air out the boat for a while and get a new solid tank before this poop deck was open for business again.

Bless his heart, he's done a lot of *shitty* jobs on this boat, but that was the smelliest. One can only avoid the poop deck for so long, luckily it freshened back up fairly quickly.

LESSON: Align with authenticity

We all have things in our lives that could be defined as a type of steaming poo. Things we avoid, ignore, and perhaps even prefer to hide in the deepest compartment of our souls. The problem with avoiding our messy stuff is that it never goes away. Instead, it festers inside until one day, often when you least expect it (or following a trauma), it explodes in your face.

Most of the time, ignoring the signs ends up making things worse.

There are a lot of reasons why we avoid our feelings and a lot of ways we do it.

Back in the day, my favorite way was drinking wine. After I stopped that, I picked up the 'ole 'putting others first' schtick. Until recently, I'd opt to help clients or friends create impactful projects, while putting my own on hold, because *someone needed my help*. You can't get a better excuse than helping others!

My heart projects always used to be last on my list of things to do, so I never had any energy left to work on them after giving everything I had to others. I felt depleted. Plus, I was miserable for not following through with what I promised myself I'd do, and on poured the guilt and shame. Eventually, self-anger ensued because my life wasn't the way I wanted it to be. So, I felt even worse, and I hid away even more, avoiding everything even more!

It's one of the reasons why my books took so long to write. I avoided looking at my issues, by concentrating on others. This book series requires honesty and authenticity, to share intimate details about my life, and necessitates letting go of a lot of fears and judgments I have about myself. Inner chatter and limiting beliefs like, "I'm not worthy," "Who am I to publish a book," "I don't have enough certifications," "I'll be ridiculed," "What I say doesn't matter," etc. Fears of being judged, or criticized often scare us from our goals.

From the moment I realized this, I looked at my behavior and embraced who I was without guilt, I had become a procrastinator who didn't think she deserved to, or was good enough to follow her heart. It was painful to stop avoiding looking at my messy feelings. I cried a lot at some of the things I discovered about myself, especially that I didn't think I was enough, good enough, bright enough, educated enough, experienced enough, fill-in-the-blanks enough...ENOUGH!!!

And yes, some days I felt like...well, *shit*. I wanted to change—so I did. I stopped avoiding myself and looked closely at my bad habits. I won't lie, it sucked at first; scrutinizing my actions under a bright light. Still, I committed to my word, and aligned my priorities so that I finally put myself first.

When I aligned myself with my authentic self and what I truly wanted to create in this world, I stopped avoiding.

The ways you choose to escape and avoid (TV, games, social media, work, drugs, sex, shopping, etc.) are creating imbalances in your chakras. There is no light without darkness, no highs without lows, no balance without both sides—we need the yin and the yang.

Whatever situation you are ignoring is creating friction in your life. Deep down, you already know that it will potentially end in an explosive situation. Using that knowing, bring your situation up to the surface and examine it with compassion, rather than judgment.

Our ability to communicate authentically resides in the throat, our fifth chakra. Our communication center is empowered by deep listening and authentic action aligned with our inner core. Accepting who we truly are and being able to express it accurately helps us face the stinky stuff in our lives. Be honest with yourself and know your triggers, habits, and patterns. Engaging with your messy feelings will smooth out and heal the painful edges.

QUESTION: What do I avoid, or ignore?

 ACTION: Try EFT tapping.

Emotionally Freedom Technique (EFT), developed by Gary Craig in the 1990s is an excellent and easy mind-body tool to help you learn to self-regulate, break free from bad habits, resolve issues, and release stress. Voicing affirmations out loud will also promote your fifth chakra, activate your neural pathways, and stimulate your brain.

Using your fingertips, you tap in sequence (minimum of seven times), along eight acupuncture points on meridian lines* that are located on the hands, face, and torso. While you tap, you focus on what you're trying to resolve, and you vocalize statements about that. As an energy-sensitive, Reiki teacher, I have felt EFT's powerful effects.

---

* Meridian lines are passageways in the body through which energy flows. Chakras bring and regulate energy and meridians distribute that energy throughout the body.

Browse online to learn the specific sequence and acupoints.

Example of EFT statements recited while tapping:

Even though I _____ *(insert specific event or core issue you would like to work on**)* _____, I deeply and completely love, and accept myself.

**Sample language to help fill in the line, and complete the exercise above:

- am frustrated with being sick again
- feel disconnected with my partner
- struggle with my body image

5. Dancing in the Galley— The Circle of Life

Align your Timing

"If you dance with the waves, they will give you the world."
—*Carole*

Fixing meals can be an acrobatic feat on high seas. I'm not talking about cooking at anchor with the occasional waves and continuous bobbing. I'm referring to feeding an exhausted crew when the boat is sailing on top of an 8-foot wave in one moment—then dropping down to the bottom in the next. I'm talking about heeling at a 45-degree angle, standing sideways in rough seas with no respite regardless of what you're cooking. And for serious offshore sailors, this ain't even close to high seas!

My husband has always been amazed at my capacity to be downstairs in stormy seas. You'd think that it's the safest place to be, but 90 percent of people get seasick when they go below in bad weather. Sensitive stomachs can't handle the crazy swinging of the environment. Our brains are used to stable ground, and unmoving scenery. Our eyes and ears can acclimate to sailing, but turbulent seas will bring the level of motion to a new high.

Seasickness is caused when there is a disturbance in the inner ear, and you can't visualize anything stable. Repeated motions will make you lose your sense of balance and equilibrium, and likely your most recent meal. The brain panics and makes you nauseous. Looking at the horizon will sometimes stabilize motion sickness. Take away one's ability to lock on a stable view, and there'll be projectile flying all over the boat. Usually, fresh air will help people keep it under control, so we always kept our guests upstairs in the cockpit on choppy seas.

Below deck is a different world. Sailboats are made to heel and withstand a lot of motion. The shelves have a lip to keep items from falling off. Extra tie-downs lock larger objects in place. Cabinets and doors have latches to stay closed—nothing is simply left hanging, free to move. Glass holders, hooks, non-slip rugs, and Velcro are your best friends. We avoided buying glass items, opting to use plastic, acrylic, or Corelle in the kitchen.

Even though we were in an environment where the floor and walls were built to accommodate life at an angle, movement was still restricted. Our cozy interior could turn into a moving circus.

Everything I needed for cooking, eating, entertaining, and navigating for several months, was stowed in a room that was approximately 13 feet wide, 15 feet long, and 7 feet high. That was the space of our galley-salon area (galley is the kitchen, salon is the living room/dining room). Picture the whole room moving up and down, you'll feel the motion in your stomach and heart, just like on a carnival ride, your guts sink one second and then rise up another. Add to that the angle of the boat—a sailboat always moves at an angle because of the wind in the sails. So, we were heeling either to portside (left) or starboard side (right), depending on our direction, and on top of that, there was a certain amount of swinging back and forth with every incoming wave.

Through the many portholes (small windows on the side of the boat), I saw the grey cloudy sky one second, and underwater bubbles the next. Once in a while, I could see and hear a wave crashing on top of the boat, over my head, spraying saltwater over the closed hatches. When there was a lot of spray, I'd have a few salty drops come down the companionway (ladder/stairs leading to the cockpit) beside me.

Chapter 5 — Align your Timing

The clashing and banging of every item onboard was intrusive. Layered into this was the normal creaking sound of a sailing ship. As the wind howled in the sails, there was an underlying WOOOOO, SWISHHHHHH, SPALSHHHHHH, BRRRRR, a constant vibration and clanging from the stays down the mast. This was Windsong, in his happy place, dancing and singing with the wind and waves.

And I was the maestro of the galley. Listening to the sounds and movement of this orchestra, and dancing along with it. I cannot not move. Whatever I reached for to hold on to would move away, but if I was patient, it would also roll back to me on the next wave. Everything was moving—the floor, ceiling, walls, myself! Even when I sat, I would have to hold on with my legs and arms to stay in place.

This was my galley, and my mission (when I chose to accept it)—to feed the unsettled stomachs of my crew upstairs. Because I had the fortune of not getting seasick, I was always the designated chef and go-getter in less-than-perfect sailing conditions. That meant every time someone needed something downstairs that took a certain amount of time, other than bathroom trips, I was elected.

First, to dance in the galley, I needed good dancing shoes. At any signs of weather, I put on good boat shoes or Tevas®, as my footing was the only thing keeping me from dangerous slipups, bruises, or a wet trip overboard. My galley floor was only 1-1/2ft x 3-1/2ft and enclosed on three sides by a half wall, counter, and stove. Being so small, it was easy to secure myself with a wide stance, squeezing one foot against the side of the stairs, and the other against the other corner. There was even a hook screwed in front of the double kitchen sink, if I chose to tie my harness to it, but it never came to that.

The next thing I needed was to learn the moves and the steps. One moment my left hip was high above and all my weight was on the right leg, and the next it was down below where my right shoulder used to be, and I swung my body all the way to my left. I alternated bending the left knee, then the right knee, swinging my hips forward and aft, and getting into some kind of balance with the motion. The more chaotic the seas, the quicker the steps, and the more bumps I did. Bend, stretch, step, bump.

I would never be able to dance for long if I didn't find the rhythm. You see, the ocean has a song, and in order to master the dance, you must listen and count the steps. One wave, two waves, three for sure. Medium wave, tuck and sway a little more. Four, five, six waves move on. Large wave, heeling deeper, pausing all activity, heaving to, adding a slight suspension…theeeeeen seeeeven waves. Resume. Eight, a mega wave hits—large step, drop the knife and use both hands to hold on and secure the meal. Then start over from count one. There was also the occasional rogue wave, which I could not account for, but the captain usually saw them coming and gave me a warning. If I could count, I could dance, and could anticipate what the boat would do. There is always a rhythm in the waves, just as there is always a rhythm in dancing with life.

Once I learned how to dance, everything else fell into place.

I learned to synchronize opening the fridge, and jars, along with the moves of the boat. I would reach for condiments when the waves heeled to starboard so they were snuggled against the hull rather than crashing on the floor. I'd put sharp knives in the sink when not using them, and always made sure I knew what cycle the waves were in before opening jars or cupboards. Items slipped and slid inside cabinets with each wave, hence the no glass rule on the boat!

The only way to keep our mayo and plates from sliding left to right on the counter was anti-slip placemats. I put them everywhere. Yes, certain unsecured items escaped on occasion, typically ending up in the kitchen sink as the counter had a lip. I avoided liquids when possible, otherwise the floor could get messy.

Making sandwiches for lunch was easy. I remember making spaghetti in a small craft weather advisory, that's 5 - 7 foot seas. I was tired of cold meals while cruising a bad weather system and decided to cook a hot meal for everyone. Our stove was a standard 2-burner propane gimbaled stove. It remained in a locked position when docked, but when cooking in rough seas, I could unlock it and let it swivel along with the boat. As the boat heaved to, the stove was free to swing back and forth, staying leveled with gravity, rather than following the waves and spilling the content of the pans. As long as I had deep pots and pans, I was able to keep the contents secured inside. Each stove range had adjustable potholders—two little arms that moved to capture the cauldron and locked it into place so that it remained over the fire while the stove swung.

It was quite something to see and not your typical onboard experience, cooking while the waves were throwing me around, holding myself as best as I could, dancing, chopping, holding on, swinging to the rhythm of the boat, my body going up and down like on a roller coaster, while I was being careful to cut the carrots and not my fingers AND doing this as my stove gimballed back and forth beside me with water boiling for pasta and spaghetti sauce cooking over an open flame! I usually did this while singing songs and holding a friendly conversation with my guests looking down at me from the cockpit.

On occasion, the captain would holler, "Boat!" or "Wave!" That meant stop everything and hang on for dear life because incoming waves from a passing vessel would soon rock the boat, or a larger rogue wave was going to hit. For those, I needed to pause what I was doing—from down below I never knew how big the wake was, or how much we would roll—and saving dinner was my priority (after my safety of course).

I rarely felt woozy cooking in the galley, and I spent a lot of time preparing meals in bad weather. I sometimes thought there must have been something wrong with my inner ear, as everyone who casually offered to help would quickly run back upstairs, green, and sweaty. I kept my breath long and steady, and my mind occupied on the task at hand. It has always helped me stay focused. Was it comfortable? Not really. Did I wish I would be anchored quietly? Of course! Did I have a choice in the matter? Not if I wanted a hot meal! So, what did I do? I made do, put a smile on my face, and fed my crew. And if it got too hot, I popped outside for a breath of fresh air.

Once I learned how to dance this sea rumba, I could dance anywhere and under any circumstances.

LESSON: Align your timing

Learning to dance in the galley is a great allegory to learning to dance with the rhythm and cycles of life. What do you do when everything around you moves so fast that you can't get a clear picture, don't have anyone to hold on to, or have a stable pot to piss in (couldn't resist!)? You breathe. You breathe and you focus on the task at hand. You become present in the movement. You find the rhythm, find your center, and learn to dance with the elements.

Deep inside of you is a place where nothing moves, nothing can harm you, nothing is scary and the light always points you back to Source, like an inner compass. Find your center and breathe into it. From this calm center, you can observe life around you, and start seeing patterns and cycles. Everything has a rhythm, a beat, a flow—if you pay attention. You can adapt and fall into rhythm with what is around you, even if only temporarily. If you don't like the patterns you are seeing, guess what? You are the captain of your ship, and you can change direction! You can steer your life to whatever rhythm you like. There is absolutely no one stopping you, except you, unless you let someone commandeer your ship. If

Chapter 5 — Align your Timing

you find yourself dancing to someone else's rhythm and you don't like it—stop it and learn new steps.

We all go through rough patches where we need to hang on. It's okay to not be comfortable, breathe into your center, find your peace, and project calm seas all around you. Go with the flow, observe, and make the necessary adjustments to change your course.

Be mindful of timing; step in rhythm with life, otherwise, you may get kicked off the dance floor.

On a deeper yogic level, everything is energy, hence everything is waves and frequencies. The wave is never-ending in time. Recognize your position on the wave. You may be on a peak, or you may be on your way down the valley. Wherever you are, it will eventually carry you back to the flow. Learn to recognize and appreciate which part of the cycle you are in. It is soothing to know that we are part of nature and affected by cycles just like every other living thing.

Women's Cycle
As women, we have a deeper connection with cycles because of our menses. We are intrinsically connected with our sisters, our cycles even synchronize when living with other women.

After my hysterectomy,* I was overjoyed to be a part of the, "White panty club" as my OBGYN called it, but at the same time felt a deeper unexplainable loss. I never wanted children, yet I felt that I had lost something precious. Had the scalpel cut away part of my being that was vital for my wholesomeness? I longed for what had been there and felt a void, not only in my empty womb but deep in my essence. With two healthy ovaries remaining, I counted days and kept track of my cycles on a calendar for as long as I could.

Some months I could tell it was coming by the influx of hormones, mood swings, and fatigue. But it got harder and harder to keep track without bleeding as some months went by without any physical signs.

I'd spent a whole day cleaning Windsong, washing the dog, polishing the rails, and then realized the following day as I lay on the settee exhausted and aching that the extra influx of energy had been announcing the coming of my cycle.

Eventually, I integrated energy practices in my life—like reiki, Shakti Dance®, and visualizations—that helped me heal the energetic wound the operation left behind. I learned to observe the even subtler signs my body was giving me and to be even more attentive to my energy cycle.

With the ebb and flow of our periods, women are gifted with signs of when to be active and when to rest. We can use this knowledge to our advantage by booking important events and meetings when we feel at our best, and making time for retreats when we need to rest.

In the winter of our lives, we must honor our hormones and how they affect our mood and health and find balance as we move through our day.

There is also a time to create, with the waxing moon, and a time to let go, with the waning moon. Offer a pause during the new moon and simply be present to honor the great cycle governing it all, dance, and celebrate when the moon is at its fullest.

*(See book #1)

QUESTION: What areas of my life feel out of balance? What areas feel on solid ground?

 ACTION: Personal year numerology

Knowing where you are in your personal numerology year can help you understand what challenges may be going on in your life. From birth to death, we go through a cycle every nine years. There is a particular energy relating to each year within the cycle.

This doesn't mean that you can only start a new career in a personal year 1, it's just that the energies are focused and supportive of it. It's a fun way to keep track of your cycles of life and be more aware of underlying currents that guide it.

To figure out which of the year cycles and energy you are in now, add your birth month to your birth day and to the year we are currently in. Keep adding each single number until you are left with only a one-digit number.

Ex.: If your birthday is July 18 and the current year is 2023:

0+7+1+8+2+0+2+3 = 23

then 2 + 3 = 5

Your current Personal Year is 5.

Meanings :

Year 1: New Beginnings

Year 2: Relationships & Partnership

Year 3: Social life, Creativity & Self-expression

Year 4: Self-Improvement & Stability

Year 5: Changes & Personal Freedom

Year 6: Home Life & Responsibilities

Year 7: Self-reflection & Growth

Year 8: Abundance & Reward (Karma)

Year 9: Completion of Cycle & Letting Go

Personal year numerology stops at 9. But, occasionally you may find that you get the number of 11. If so, do not add the 1+1, just keep the master number 11. It's a rare occurrence and considered a blessing.

Year 11: Inspiration, Intuition & Spirituality

6. 911—When Stuck—Save the Popsicles

Align Patience with Positivity

Eric with his daughter, Sarah.

"When stuck, find the cool sweetness." —Carole

As high of a rush as a sailing day could be, you could also end up high and dry.

It was the first time that we were taking Eric's kids, daughter age 10 and son 12, sailing for their summer vacation. By this time, Eric and I had lived aboard for a little over a year and the kids, who lived with their mom in Canada, had gone on day sails at spring break and other holidays but this was their initiation to leaving the dock overnight for several days and sailing offshore to the Florida Keys.

The Keys—or Cays—are a stretch of approximately 800 islands extending over 198 miles at the southern tip of Florida.

We had been boasting about how much fun we would have snorkeling, traveling to all kinds of places, and seeing sea life of all shapes, sizes, and colors, in water clearer than they'd ever seen. I could only imagine how exciting and exotic this must have seemed in the mind of a landlubbing child.

It was an uneventful trip sailing approximately 100 nautical miles south and we spent the last few days at anchor, cruising and exploring the bays, chasing lobsters, and going on dinghy rides with Dingo, the family dog. We decided to spend the night at a marina to refuel, refill our water tanks, and take the kids on a well-deserved outing to explore the laid-back island town.

I typically was the chart plotter on duty, but it was lunchtime, and I was down below making sandwiches for everyone when the captain decided to veer to starboard and cut through the bay aiming the boat directly at the entrance of the marina far away in the distance. I felt the floor below my feet rub against the bottom of the sea. It was a forceful grinding halt but not life-threatening. Damn. We were aground. Again. I used to call my husband "Captain Sandbar" because he liked to venture out without paying much attention to the charts, and often placed us in gritty situations. The waters in the Keys were very shallow. You had to be careful where you navigated because many areas had seagrass which was protected because of its importance in supporting the ecosystem; small species lived and depended on it to thrive. The conservation efforts led by many organizations were reinforced by the presence of Park Rangers. If you didn't know the area, it was best to stay within the channels or navigate very carefully when outside the markers. Just because you saw water everywhere, didn't mean there was room for your vessel to roam.

Eric was definitely a color-outside-the-lines type of guy, and we were outside of the channel. Distracted by the kids and eager to dock in port after days at anchor, he hadn't noticed that we entered a protected area. I got the binoculars, and we could see a small sign outside of the waterway in the back of us. We were grounded on a sandy dune, so he tried to put the motor in reverse and stab it at full speed. Not even a budge. We all jumped on the same side of the boat, trying to "shake" us off (good luck with a 15+ ton boat!). We ran forward and aft at full speed, but nothing. Veering starboard and port side, forward and reverse with all of Windsong's might, and we didn't even budge one inch. We were parked on a bump.

A boat was coming toward us at full speed from the marina entrance. Eric got his hands off the steering wheel and sat down.

Chapter 6 — Align Patience with Positivity

The Park Ranger was on us within a few minutes, circling us in his open skiff. The kids popped their heads up from down below and Eric told them, "Not a word you two!"

"What are you doing?" The ranger asked.

"We're stuck," Eric answered.

"This is a protected area. You can't power off the bottom or you'll get fined. You have to wait for high tide to float free or get towed off." The ranger warned.

"I understand, no problem," Eric replied.

"Then why is your motor running?" the ranger asked, eyeing him suspiciously.

"To keep the popsicles cold for the kids, sir." Captain said.

This was a partly true and fully quick comeback captain, and witty!

Even though it was sand where we were, the law specified that we had to wait for high tide before we would be allowed to use the motor to break free, and that's only if we were still stuck. There was seagrass close by which was protected. Eric told him we had the motor on to keep the freezer cold, and we would stay there until we'd float free. Damaging aquatic seagrass preserves could carry penalties in the thousands of dollars. That bought a lot of popsicles.

Bloody hell! The tide was on its way down, not up! That meant that it wasn't even at its lowest yet—we would have to wait for hours for the tide to hit its height, and then lower. For now, it would continue its cycle of grounding us even further before it would rise back up, get back to where it was now, and then rise even more, hopefully releasing us on its own accord when enough water would allow us to finally float away. It was going to be a very….long….day.

Mister Ranger would have his binoculars glued on us the whole time, like a shark stalking his prey, hoping to sneak a speedy ambush after sensing movement or blood. We weren't going to let one drop of tension create waves in the waters today; we settled in for a long haul and played dead.

From that moment on it was a waiting game in 90+ degree heat. We were getting baked with no wind and disappointing two landlubbing kids on their first sailing vacation. There we sat, stuck on an underwater sand dune—without technology—for hours.

It was so beautifully foreign to them. Their first time in the amazing Keys and they couldn't even go anywhere, as if they were grounded. DUH, WE ALL WERE!! Grounded for not paying attention.

Low tide was predicted at 15h00 and high tide was expected around 20h30, after sunset. It was an excruciating wait for my husband who suffers from extreme impatientness. There was nothing we could do, the ranger stationed himself at the entrance of the marina and patrolled the bay all day.

There are two types of grounding in boating—a soft grounding and a hard one. A soft grounding is when you land on a bed of sand, rarely causing any damage to the boat, but causing many headaches to get free depending on how hard you ran aground, wind directions, waves, etc. Soft groundings stop you dead on your path and are an inconvenient annoyance, but you come out of it unscathed.

A hard grounding is when you land on rocks or reefs. You do not want to be in this position. The damage can be devastating, and irreparable (I have a few stories to tell about such groundings). Most of the time, both groundings can be avoided by paying close attention to all surroundings.

In Florida and the Bahamas, there are semidiurnal tides which means there are two high waters (high tides) and two low waters (low tides) each tidal day. A complete tide cycle, high and low, is 12 hours and 25

Chapter 6 — Align Patience with Positivity

minutes, so there are two a day, or specifically every 24 hours and 50 minutes. Hence, the time of the tide changes every day and you must keep a watch on local tide charts as you travel.

Since we were parked on waterfront property, we cranked up the Bob Marley and Eric Stone island tunes and instead of eating on the go, I prepared a pretty darn good lunch. We installed the cockpit table and picnicked at our new beach front condo. And yes, the kids even had their popsicles!

Some people would have paid a lot of money to have a nice picnic like ours, floating tranquility aboard a sailboat with a beautiful view of the island, clear water, and tropical weather. One's perspective could be very different depending on whether you were there by choice, by force or stuck into it.

Eric could not stay in one place for too long, it drove him nuts! His therapist called him a wanderlust. He was always on the move so being forced to stay in one place, not by his choice, was an exercise of extreme patience. Especially knowing that we were being watched all day.

Second worst, behind the wait, was the sun. You couldn't escape it. It was so hot that you couldn't walk barefoot on the deck or you'd burn the sole of your feet—even us serious barefooters! There wasn't a cloud in the sky and the stifling heat suffocated any air movement. Since we had entered a small bay, we were sheltered from any sea breeze that would have come from the east. We were getting sunburned in the cockpit, and it was so hot you couldn't breathe down below. We resorted to hanging towels and sheets around the sunny side of the cockpit to create shade while simultaneously applying immeasurable amounts of sunscreen. We watched the minutes pass and the tide lower at an excruciatingly slow pace.

When we ran out of jokes and stories to tell each other we decided that if we were going to be stuck in shallow clear waters, we might as well take advantage of it and get in it. We got everyone equipped with masks, snorkels, fins, and scrapers, and put Eric and the kids to work scrubbing the bottom.

The bottom of a boat needs to be scrubbed free of barnacles regularly. Those are little marine crustaceans that grow on boat hulls in the warm salt waters of the south. They attach themselves permanently to surfaces like whales, lobsters, rocks, boat bottoms, pilings, etc., and grow their shells directly onto them, feeding by filtering particles in the water around them. It's a nuisance for boats, slowing down the speed of the boat by replacing the smooth gliding surface with rough resistance on the water. Their sharp carapace easily cuts the skin, making your climb on the swimming platform potentially bloody. They clog thru-hulls (a fitting from holes in a boat's hull that allow water intake or outtake for sea cock, motor cooling, knotmeter (speed water gauge), or efficiencies like sink water runoff, etc.). In the south, a monthly hull scrubbing was necessary, and in the summertime, they grew at amplified speed.

Sarah was surprised at seeing so much underwater life on the bottom of her dad's boat. No one thought that there could be anything growing there except algae. *(Fun fact: We sometimes heard sea turtles or coral fish nibble on the growth on the bottom of our boat.)*

The water was cool and clear until they started scraping then the discarded bits and pieces clouded the water creating a perfect buffet for hundreds of little fishes who took advantage of the free meal.

So, we were stuck between a marina and a soft place with our vacation temporarily on hold. Or, was it? We weren't moving but we had fun making the most of it. We played games, danced, played hangman—funny the words kids can come up with—got a deck of cards and played a few rounds. There was nothing else to do but relax.

It was now four o'clock. We spent the day doing all that we could to entertain the kids and keep everyone cool—both literally and figuratively. We saw the Ranger patrol the bay on a few occasions. Other boats sailed by while we sat unmoving, high and dry on the sand bank. We saw families hauling kids on floaties sail by, fishermen went out, returning hours later suntanned, and with coolers filled with the day's catch. We saw happy couples strolling by in skiffs. Sailboats returned from day sails, and cormorants circled around us, wondering if we were a new permanent fixture in the bay's scenery.

We were all tired of the unusually-even-for-Florida-hot-burning-sun as if we'd been put under cooking lamps or the blinding light of an interrogator before being forced to walk on hot coals.

Then we saw the sunset cruises come out. We were STILL STUCK. Surrounded by water, a lone sailboat at the entrance of the bay in front of a horizon of water and a panoply of red, oranges, and yellows. The only good thing about the sun setting was that it finally cooled down a bit. When the sunset cruisers came back in, we were just about done.

At 20h00 a marine patrol checked on us again, I wondered if they changed shifts and notified the newcomer to keep an eye on us. We hadn't planned on sleeping out there but the good thing about living on a boat was that it didn't matter where you were, everywhere you went, there was your home.

The tide finally turned! With the incoming rush of water, we were hopeful that we wouldn't have to call in an expensive Sea-Tow so late in the game to drag us off. They were expensive. We could tell that Windsong had regained some buoyancy from the way it felt less heavy and more upright, but it took a long time until the waves that hit us started to actually cause our boat to rock.

The sun had set when we started to feel the boat slide a bit.

"Oh, are we moving? What was that? Did we move?" We all screamed. I'd never been this excited about a bob before.

"I'm not sure, I can't tell but we're close, let's get ready." Eric said.

It was dark. We were salty, sunbaked, tired, and oh-so-ready for anything to happen.

Slowly but surely, we felt the ocean loosen its grip and our heart fluttered with each rocking wave becoming bigger and bigger.

"We're floating!" Hold on, this is it. We're going to go any second now. "We're moving! We're MOVING!!!!!!!! Go, go, GO! YAYYYY!" Maximum speed reverse, to back off the hump, then back from where we came in to re-enter the channel. All four of us screamed with joy! "Finally, we're free!"

At 21h30, we floated free of the sandbar. Released from limbo, we got back on our now very well-planned trajectory; sailing northeast then veering into the marina for the night to blast our thick-blooded Canadian kids with some cold A/C. We'd had enough of an unmoving adventure for the day!

 LESSON: Align patience with positivity (and always keep popsicles in the freezer!)

It's funny because I got stuck while writing this chapter, and as soon as I saw myself staring blankly at the screen, I stopped, got up, grabbed the leash, and walked toward the companionway. My furry sidekick, always ready to get off board, was ready for a walk. He jumped into my arms, and I lifted and lowered him into the cockpit, then pulled the lines so the boat floated closer to the dock, and he jumped off. There was so much enthusiasm and joy in his step, tail wagging, crying a bit, and running in circle while he waited for me to jump off, he had the biggest happy grin.

The instant that I relaxed and enjoyed being with my little guy—whose life revolves around the present moment—I felt grounded and connected and stopped stressing about what to write and the words started to flow. (So much that I wished I had brought a notepad on my walk!)

We often feel stuck when we are forced into "doing mode" versus "being mode." We are hard on ourselves and pushing for something to happen instead of being patient and embracing the pause.

Those moments when filled with patience, openness, and positivity can bring valuable insights, rest, and cherished moments as we enjoy being present.

There is much to be learned from being stuck. The timing may not be right. Maybe you're going too fast and need to slow down so the universe forces you into a resting period. Source has a way of slowing us down when it's trying to communicate with us. When we feel stuck—we are usually out of alignment.

Most of us have felt stuck at one point or another. Some of us may feel stuck right now. We may not know what our next step is, what we want to do in life, or what to do about a challenge. It feels like life is moving forward without us, leaving us behind with a huge case of FOMO (Fear of Missing Out). We see everyone else enjoying life, but we're stuck isolated on a sandbar with no idea how to get "back in the game."

I learned from all the times I felt stuck, to be patient and grateful. Patient with myself for being in this position, and patient with others who may have contributed to my situation. Grateful that things could be worse and trusting for the best possible outcome. It's okay to just BE.

I used to fuss a lot about being in limbo and put myself under an incredible amount of pressure for not having it all figured out. Life taught me to relax and use this time to play, do things I enjoy, and allow time for creative thinking. Eventually, I would intuitively feel what next step I needed to take.

Being stuck is the perfect time to self-reflect, rest and recharge, process and integrate events we've lived through, or refocus our priorities. It is in rest mode, in a stress-free environment that inspiration naturally guides us back into alignment and gets us moving again. Say yes to being stuck!

And even if you feel like you might be stuck, know that every single thing in this universe is in constant motion so even if you don't see it, the Universe has you moving toward something and is conspiring to release you back in the flow when the timing is right. So, enjoy the……….pause. Be okay with not knowing, embrace the moment, and let life surprise you.

QUESTION: The next time I feel stuck, I will...

 ACTION: Creative playtime

The next time you feel stuck in life or need to brainstorm a challenge, schedule some creative playtime into your day. Even if you feel you are not the artistic type, spend time coloring, doing paint-by-number, beading, sewing, painting rocks (leave them hidden in beaches and sites you visit!), building birdhouses, making jewelry, or anything that helps you tap into your creative side. It's not about the end result but activating the right side of the brain which is responsible for creative thinking, inspiration, and intuition. It will unlock energies untapped by your left-sided logical brain and offer intuitive options to get in the flow again.

7. Night Navigation—Blinded I Seek

Align Actions with Intuition

"A well-tuned inner compass will never fail. Instruments will." —Carole

We'd been running nonstop for 48 hours. Sailing as hard as we could to get away from the monster tropical depression that was creeping over the Bahamian island chain. We'd gotten stuck for three days hiding in a deserted cove on the southeast side of Andros because I could not take the pitch and polling of the boat and begged Eric to find a place to anchor. That day, for the first time in my sailing life, I cried and tied myself to the helm of Windsong. We weren't even in the middle of a hurricane; I had lived through much worse. But there was something about that storm—the smacking angle of the waves and how Windsong teetered from side to side, (burying its toe rail in the messy ocean) that weakened my resolve. We'd rarely experienced such a pronounced port-to-starboard motion while sailing. Observing how close our boat sides were swinging and swaying, all the way down to water level, with every wave made me anxious. I wasn't nauseous thanks to my superhuman (or defective) eardrums, but the seas were rough, and I felt queasy in the pit of my stomach. Not in a throw-up kind of way but in a "Good God, what am I doing in the middle of this massive washing machine, please get me out of here" kind of way.

I could feel my body's center of gravity shift every time Windsong dipped and almost felt temporarily weightless as my body lifted and this ball of feelings from my gut traveled to my throat. I held on with sweaty palms and braced myself as hard as I could waiting for the boat to right itself back up. Hoping it would right itself up. We heeled so badly that if I let go, I'd possibly drop vertically in for a swim. I had never been afraid of falling off the boat before, but today I was frightened. My instincts kicked in and I put my safety harness on and snapped the tether clip around the helm's grab rail.

Eric tried to comfort me while he enjoyed the challenging sail. He was in full control of the boat and he couldn't understand the waves of fear that were overtaking me.

"We're in no danger of being knocked down, honey. We've been through much worse. The boat is handling well, and it just feels uncomfortable, it's not dangerous."

The level gauge was breaking records. It was like being on a bad carnival ride and looking below and seeing yourself freefalling smack into the water, except I was tied and couldn't get off. There was nowhere to go. It just went on and on and on. We couldn't have faced the approaching storm in the unprotected anchorage we were in the night before, so we were trying to out run Mother Nature.

My insides twisted in doom. Maybe it was seeing how easily my home and safe space was tossed around, or maybe I had lost my edge and used up all my courage fighting chronic illness.

I sat on the cockpit floor and cried. Eric couldn't let go of the wheel, but he talked to me and tried to calm me down. I pushed my back against the 3-foot-high bench seat and my legs against the lower one in front of me, to my side was the foot-high hull separating me from going down the companionway. I was somewhat stabilized from the rocking and boxed myself in by creating a small safe space where I could concentrate on getting my nerves under control. I stayed there, hiding from a view of the threatening horizon and my watery foe. Eric promised safe harbor

Chapter 7 — Align Actions with Intuition

soon but there just wasn't much that anyone could do but hold on, literally.

We were in open water sailing north over the Tongue of the Ocean, a 150-mile-long area with water depths ranging from 3,600 to 6,600 feet (1,100-2,000 meters). The waves could become massively chaotic under the right conditions, and they were. The captain commanded Windsong and mastered the elements, but my insides disagreed with this cacophony.

After that miserable afternoon, we ditched our plans and ducked for three days in a protected bay to wait out the storm so the seas—and I—would calm down. It was so rough that we couldn't even take the dinghy to explore the anchorage even though it laid inside a protective reef. Eric ventured on the last day and came back drenched saying, "This ain't no fun."

The storm left me beaten, tired, and eager to get back to our home-berth in the Florida Keys. Even though we had a phenomenal time exploring a stretch of islands in the Exumas, reality was knocking, and Eric had to be back at work managing a boatyard in just a few days so we would have to race around the clock to make up for lost time. The prospect wasn't enticing but it was time to set sail.

The morning wind was fierce, and the water was still rough but manageable. At least, Windsong now felt like normal wet sailing and not a roller coaster trying to shake us off. We ran our ketch at top speed under iron sail (engine) and full sails traveling north to round about the large island. Andros is 104 miles of mostly uninhabited land covered with forest, pine, and wildlife. Known to some as the "Bonefish Capital of the World," except for sparse friendly settlements and a few ocean research facilities, it was mostly left to its mosquito population and fly fishermen. Cruisers were warned to bring heavy-duty mosquito repellent if planning a visit. Under other circumstances, I would have loved to visit the renowned pristine blue hole and other treasures it hid.

A south passage through the flats for a boat our size without local knowledge wasn't an option in rough weather so we continued our journey north to go around the island. We had been anchored close to the South Bight, so even if we could maintain our fastest speed of 7 knots, we'd still need about 10 hours just to get to the northernmost tip. We close hauled and reached most of the day, meaning the wind was on our fore quarter leaving us to constantly steer port to starboard to keep our sails tight.

Our progress was slowed by crashing into the oncoming waves which shaved knots off our speed making our estimated landfall much later than we'd expected. The only other option was for us to wait days in the rough anchorage when the weather system was forecast to pass and pay the price with days of lost work and a very unhappy boss. (After a month, bosses tend to get antsy!)

By the time we got to the northernmost tip of the island, it was nightfall. Our ears were numb from the constant wind deafening our thoughts and the long hours of sailing against the elements were exhausting.

Being far away from any large cities meant that the nights were pitch black. We could see lights appearing everywhere between us and the shore, flickering in between the choppy waves. Knowing the Andros Great Barrier Reef lay close by, we worried about colliding with whatever was out there, and I could not find any lighted buoys or markers on the charts. We kept a sharp eye and used all our senses to figure out that they were small skiffs with fishermen coming out from the harbor. Either we had completely lost our touch and became wimpy sailors, or these islanders were nuts! Brave souls fishing in these conditions. Hopefully, being on the other side of the reef somewhat tamed the wake.

Drained from the last few days, we planned for a layover in the northernmost anchorage of Andros where a commercial harbor offered

Chapter 7 — Align Actions with Intuition

limited protection. The entrance to Morgan's Bluff was hard to find, especially after the tiring day we'd had. It was nerve-wracking not seeing where we were going and bringing our vessel that contained all our possessions—our home, ourselves, and our dog—close to shore. It felt safer out there in the deep sea. The last thing we wanted was to collide with something. The navigation signs in the islands were rudimentary and sometimes nonexistent. And when the chart said, "lighted buoy," it didn't mean that the present day matched the year that our chart was published. Crossed our fingers that they were maintained.

We finally found the post that marked the entrance channel where Windsong could safely sail through the reef. As we changed course, we felt the boat settle comfortably for the first time that day. GAWD, what a relief! We'd anchored there before and it was a bad experience. It was infamous for being exposed to northern swells and having poor holding ground. We knew that it wasn't the best place to sleep, but with the nearest island hours away, it was our only option for some shut-eye.

The only way we'd get any rest would be to bring the boat as deep as possible into the cove and hope that the wind would remain behind the small strip of land breaking the waves. We were dangerously close to the beach, so with that in mind, we had to sleep with one eye open.

Our bunk never felt this good. We got a few hours of sleep before the boat started rocking again. Eric got up and set a second anchor to stabilize the boat. The changing tide brought unwelcomed swells. It felt like we had been on board a washing machine for days with no respite from the wash cycle. I wasn't seasick, I was just sick of it. We laid in bed, half dozing and waking up every larger wave. Feet going up, head going down. Head going up, feet going down. The crease and pull and splash and heave, then WHOA, the big wave where we found ourselves half up while still lying down. Then, the cycle started over again. Too dark to leave, yet impossible to sleep, we just laid there wishing it would all stop. Eventually it calmed down and we thought the ocean was finally settling down. Just as we were on the cusp of long-awaited slumber, again the swells! Arghhhh. Torture!

As idyllic as the beginning of this trip had been, this last part of the journey taught us about endurance and resilience.

By first light we pulled out, red-eyed and cranky from the lack of sleep. We had over 130 miles ahead of us before we reached Islamorada in the Florida Keys, and we had already lost three days ducking the storm, so we had to sail back that day if Eric was to get back to work on time. Today would be a better day, I told myself.

The weather system still loomed, but we were done rounding the island and now sailed southwest. That meant that we now surfed the waves and spent the day sailing the shallow outer banks. It was an exhilarating feeling to surf on a 15-ton boat. The beating, crashing force of every wave pushing back, getting splashed, and getting slowed down by oncoming seas, was replaced. Now, we were now carried, supported, and pushed toward our destination. It was sunny and dry, with beautiful wind to spare.

We made great headway, sailing nonstop toward our goal, the South Riding Rocks just north of Orange Cay. This waypoint was where we would leave Bahamian waters and enter international waters on our way back to the US. Behind us was the storm and wicked TOTO (Tongue of the Ocean). The sail would be smooth and although we could not click our heels to get home, we could relax, lick our wounds, and push on.

That afternoon, we had the thrill of sailing with a large pod of dolphins. The porpoises swam left, right, under, and raced alongside us. It was sublime! They followed us for hours and took turns riding our bow wake, jumping in front of us, and showing off their prowess as they frolicked in playfulness. I sat on the bow captured by them, reaching my hand down and almost touching them. Our eyes locked gaze, our joyfulness and curiosity for each other made us instant friends. Their speed and playfulness were extraordinary to watch. I loved to interact with dolphins in the wild. They were naturally jubilant and carefree! It was one of my favorite things about sailing and this experience made up for sailing through any storm!

Any day with a dolphin sighting was an omen of good things to come. The deep orange of the sunset touched the horizon and kissed our cheeks. This marked the last we saw of the friendly pod as darkness took hold.

We sailed on and took advantage of the weather window and extra speed gained by surfing the waves to cross back to US waters under the cover of the stars.

We had been aggressively sailing, first to outrun the storm, then to get out of the storm, then to reach safe anchorages, and now to get back home in the fastest and shortest distance, which doesn't always translate well in sailing. Fortunately, this day saw the ocean finally lay down and a sense of peace permeated everything.

By the time we reached our waypoint (a waypoint is a precise latitude and longitude position where you typically change course), it was pitch dark and we couldn't see a thing—a recurring theme.

The South Riding Rock was a reef and rock formation that marked the end of the shallow banks and the beginning of the deep ocean. It was a very exposed area miles away from any type of protection in the middle of nowhere. On the other side sat the Straits of Florida. 82 miles west was Carysfort lighthouse offshore of Key Largo, 296 miles south was Cuba, and 18 miles north was the small island of Gun Cay.

We were a tiny boat, looking for a tiny dot on an ocean of water. But underwater, its chasms, dangerous shoals, peeks, and sharp reefs threatened vessels. There was a ridge of rocks and shoals going north and south for miles, with giant corral heads, some protruding out only at low tide, and low-lying rock islands covered with sparse brush. It was very important that we find the marked channel where it was safe to sail through, so we wouldn't crash, get stuck, or worse— sustain damage and sink, especially since we never sailed in this area, not even in the light of day.

It was a moonless night and we would be doing it in blind darkness.

The guidebook said there was a navigation light at the entrance of the channel, but we never saw one. Either it was broken, or we were completely off course which meant that we were attempting to cross the reef in the dark at the wrong place. It added a little more stress to keep us on our toes. This was shortly after GPS was unscrambled by the military and no one had learned to fully trust their accuracy yet.

The busted light didn't surprise us but it made our journey much more precarious. We'd have to proceed at extremely low speed, use all our wits, and call on our intuition to guide us.

The chart said that we could expect 15 feet of water in the middle of the channel at our current tide. So, if we remained at our lowest speed, we could "feel" our way with our depth gauge, and with the help of our GPS, which we trusted only to a certain point. We could tentatively know where we were on the chart based on the depth sounder and notation on the chart. We prayed we didn't have a rocky encounter. If the depth started to rise dramatically, we knew we were too close to shallows and veered away. The problem was, if we were off even by a few degrees, we could collide with low-lying rocks that would rise up abruptly without giving us a warning or hit underwater reefs prominent in this area and in seconds we'd be doomed and crash. So, we preceded in absolute silence with all our senses wide-opened, even the little hairs on our arms stood at attention, maneuvering in whispers and human sonic radar.

It was scary to move like this. When we were just about there, I quietly moved to the bow while Eric steered and tried to detect shades of darkness or any changes in sound, light, or sensation.

I swore I could feel the rocks out there despite being blind to our surroundings. It was so eerie, like their presence resonated with a solid echo, while the rest of the space felt fluid around it. I felt like Neo playing outside *The Matrix* for the first time and could almost feel the warm energy bouncing off the rocks from the heat of the day. The space felt different somehow, but I could not describe it in any other way than having the strong sense that we had reached the passage.

Deep breaths and in utter silence we glided through.

The depth finder started to drastically climb up, "Hurray!"

We never saw a damn thing. Whether we crossed at the right place or not, we now entered the largest playground on earth and the safety of the deep ocean. Pretty soon, we were sailing over hundreds of fathoms of water (1 fathom = 6 feet).

We snuck like bandits, stealing the treasure in the dead of the night and could now run our ketch full sails for an overnight crossing. Our human eyes had been completely useless in the dark, but our inner radar never failed us.

LESSON: Align your actions with your intuition

Our intuition resides in what's referred to as our, "third eye" which is our sixth chakra, located in the middle of our forehead. It is the greatest navigation tool for maneuvering through life. Learn to develop and trust it.

Stress & Fear—When you're stressed or tired, your nerves get frazzled and fear can overtake you, affecting judgment and clarity of mind which can put you in danger if you need to spring into action for any reason.

Stress and anxiety kill intuition. If you find yourself in the middle of a storm, remember to breathe and find a safe space to get centered and calm your emotions. Navigate what is going on inside by deciphering what is real and what is projected by the mind.

When coming from a place of calm, intuitive awareness, your actions become powerful and productive.

Waypoint—When you're trying to reach a destination, you don't necessarily need to know every detail of the journey ahead of time. All you need to know is your destination (goal), the next waypoint on your journey (next milestone), and start moving toward it. Take action, create movement aligned with it.

To do that, use your intuition to guide you and listen—even if what you are seeing, hearing, or urged to do doesn't make sense—embrace the gut feelings. The more you move with it, the more powerful your intuition becomes.

Resistance—Why fight? Why push? Success can be smooth and easy like surfing. Resistance equals an unpleasant ride. Maybe it's time to pause, assess, and steer away. When I feel resistance, I ask myself if it's time to take another route.

Flow—When we were beating into the wind and waves, we made hard progress, sacrificing comfort and a bit of safety, sometimes even putting ourselves in a bit of jeopardy. Through it all, we tried to follow the flow, surfing through the waves. With that, the sun blessed us the whole day, as did the dolphins! We were able to rest because the ride went with ease and grace. When we arrived at our destination we were able to calmly assess and move through the obstacles using our fine-tuned senses.

Senses—Intuition is informed by our five senses, insights, gut feelings, instincts, inner voice, and auric sensitivities. Intuition is a gift our ancestors were highly attuned to. Today, it seems intuition has been left to dissipate behind the more favored of 'voices' of science and technology. We each possess a highly sensitive system of sensory input—that when fine-tuned correctly will guide our way. Tap into your senses by paying attention. Notice when the hairs on your arm stand up, when your stomach feels uneasy, when you experience a light feeling of ecstasy or an uncontrollable urge to go in a certain direction. These experiences give you clues as to which action is best for you to take in that moment. And, life is happening moment to moment.

Your intuition is your greatest guide. Do not question your first impulses. Let go of any desire to analyze, rationalize, or explain it. Trust your inner voice, act, and observe the magic you create!

QUESTION: These are the ways my intuition manifests…

ACTION: 7 ways to develop your intuition

1. **Listen:** Your inner voice (intuition) is subtle and can come in the form of a thought, image, voice, physical sensation, or emotion. Pay attention.

2. **Meditate:** It improves your ability to be present and self-aware.

3. **Journal:** Ask questions and answer them automatically without pausing, let your pen roam freely and see what flows through your pen.

4. **Take chances:** Don't be afraid to act—take a chance and follow your gut feelings—even if you are unsure where it will lead. With practice you will become better at it.

5. **Act immediately:** Don't wait until your ego-mind subverts your free will. Act now.

6. **Trust:** The more you trust yourself, the more powerful your intuition will become.

7. **Let go:** Even if the outcome is not what you hoped, let go of judgment and try again. Practice makes perfect.

Next time you have a gut feeling, follow that impulse and act.

8. Sailor's Fashion—Stop Judging My Flip-Flops

Align Compassion with Humanity

"Be a rebel. Love everyone unconditionally." —Carole

Sailors have one thing in common—our love for the sea. A strong second for a lot of us is our eagerness to connect and enjoy other human company when given the opportunity.

Our introduction to potluck dinners was at our first marina. New to boating, and fresh from being land dwellers, we were eager to meet sailors and mingle with knowledgeable people. Every week, and sometimes twice a week, boaters would gather at the picnic tables either on the docks or by the marina office and connect with the small community. Everyone shared a dish, so we would have incredible spreads, and libations were often over-served. Of course, it was an excuse to meet the new sailors that had just pulled in—marinas are full of boats coming and going, all staying different lengths of time and traveling different directions—we were welcomed with open arms and felt more at home than we'd ever had before. We made friends quickly and talked with anyone willing to share knowledge with two greenhorns. Thankfully, old-timers are typically eager to tell you how it's done and talk a tall tale.

As we traveled and moved around, we recognized the same sense of community everywhere we went. The one thing I love the most about boaters is that they are friendly people. When you're out sailing, whether on a powerboat or a sailboat, you're on your own. Danger lurks close by, and you must be constantly careful and vigilant. The farther from land you go, the thicker the camaraderie. When we showed up at dusk at a new anchorage in the islands, oftentimes we'd get a welcoming committee coming by on a dinghy, inviting us to happy hour on one of the boats. We've met countless people simply by connecting in harbors or sailor's hangouts.

Most days you anchor somewhere for the night and often recognize the same boats cruising in the same area. We've struck up conversations over the VHF radio, joined strangers on their boats for cocktail hour, and partook in many awesome nights. We enjoyed connecting with other boating enthusiasts who were just as eager to go deep on topics like where we're from, where we're going, we'd exchange local knowledge, and share boating stories.

I used to be shy and self-conscious about meeting new people. Lacking self-confidence, I'd step aside and let others do the introductions. But this lifestyle has shown me that everyone is the same when you're in flip-flops. Whether you are a high-profile lawyer, bartender, boat wife, millionaire, or CEO on sabbatical; we're all floating on the same ocean, passionate about the freedom it gives us, and love to be off the grid.

We're also all at the mercy of the elements. Most of us have experienced breakdowns in the middle of the ocean and lived through some scary adventures. If you've been out there long enough, you've certainly experienced a few times when you thought you were going to die. It's not all sunsets and margaritas! Maybe the looming danger is why boaters are such a helpful tight-knit community. This is how it used to be in our towns and cities before modern society created a sense of disconnect between us and our neighbors. Nowadays most people feel like it's 'us against them.'

Here's a funny anecdote. It was post-hurricane, I don't remember which one, but it was in the late 90s in Broward County, FL and we

Chapter 8 — Align Compassion with Humanity

were docked in Hollywood. We sustained minimal damage from the Category 1 storm, but trees and power lines were down, part of our neighborhood was flooded and inaccessible, and most were without power. Until the water receded in some of the low-lying streets, we were cut off from leaving the area unless we wanted to kayak to town. Everyone around the marina was outside cleaning up and helping each other put everything back to normal when an elderly gentleman with his aide walked over looking for help. He had COPD (chronic obstructive pulmonary disease) and needed to breathe on a machine twice a day to open his airways or he would end up in the hospital. He lived alone across the street, and his nurse driving a high SUV treaded the flood waters to check-in on him and make sure that he was okay. She saw that he needed treatment but there was no electricity. It would take days before the water receded and the power would be restored, and he was panicking as to what to do to keep breathing. He had no family or friends to go to. He and his nurse went canvassing the neighborhood in search of power.

They could hear our music playing and see that the activity on our dock was business as usual despite the neighborhood being in total blackout. The aide helped the old man walk down the pier toward us. We're a friendly bunch so we struck up a conversation right away. They wondered if we had power back on, and we explained that most boaters are self-sufficient and function off the grid. When they explained to us that he needed to get his oxygen treatment, we sprung into action. Within minutes he was sitting comfortably on a patio chair on the pier with ice water in hand, and a live extension cord to plug in his nebulizer. His nurse turned on the machine. He put the clear mask over his mouth and took a deep breath. The mist hit his airways and a large smile broke over his face.

Windsong runs on three banks of 6-volt golf cart batteries and has a 2,000-watt inverter capable of supporting every necessary system on our boat. It transforms DC power (battery) into AC power (household) so we can plug in and use electricity anywhere we are as long as the batteries are charged, and this can be done by running the motor for an hour a day.

Our neighbor sat there for half an hour, breathing and asking questions about our lifestyle, curious about the boaters he saw every day from his window. He had never interacted with the boaters. We made him laugh. He was a gentle old soul and I liked him right away.

Because he needed to do his therapy twice a day, we invited him back to come as long as the power was out. So, for the next five days—this was a particularly damaging hurricane—he came every morning and late afternoon, and we'd sit with him telling stories. He was a childless widower, and his nurse was the closest thing to a family he had. He had lived quite the life but was even more enchanted to hear of our adventures. He met everyone around the marina and was genuinely surprised by the welcoming helpful community he found living right across his front lawn.

You see, the residents in this neighborhood had been battling a legal fight in court against boaters and the marina, to bar people from living aboard their boats. They claimed that boaters were a nuisance, responsible for polluting the lagoon, and their presence would lower property values, and bring up crime rates.

Simply because boaters hailed from different ports, spent most of their time in beachwear, had long hair, and looked like suntanned beach bums didn't mean that we were criminals or senseless polluters. It never crossed their minds that we were people just like them and could be even more passionate about protecting our waterways and the environment than they were. We had families, some had careers, some volunteered in the community, and despite our unconventional lifestyles, we weren't bums or low lives. The relationship between boaters and local residents wasn't very friendly, and for a select few, it was an all-out war.

The big turnaround came when one boater who lived at the marina took a water sample from the water coming out of the canal drainage pipe and had it independently analyzed. It was being dumped in the sea by the city and was spill-over from the neighborhood's storm drains and manholes. After the toxic results came in, they could not claim that boaters were the reason why the lagoon was polluted anymore, the city had to clean up its act. The fight was eventually won by the marina. Meanwhile, we had made a supportive friend for life.

After the power was restored, he gifted us with a nice bottle of wine (back then, I dabbled in such libations). Until his passing, our old neighbor became an avid reader and subscriber to our Real Sailors magazine, which we would hand deliver to his door. He continued to take occasional walks to come and say hi. He'd told all his neighbors that, "Us boaters were a nice bunch of folks," and that we had really come through for him after the storm.

Thy shall not judge a sailor by their flip-flops.

We judge what we don't know. We judge what is different. We judge what we fear. Danger and crisis make us temporarily forget about our differences because. For a short period of time, the danger shakes our brains so much that we forget our petty differences, and band together to feel stronger and safer.

Knowing that the person next door only wants to be safe, happy, and free to enjoy what they love just as much as we do, creates a bond that surpasses any social class, money, or upbringing. We see our reflection in their hopes and dreams. If we stop our critical minds and put away the judgments, we find that behind stories, clothes, and surroundings, there is a person in front of us who only wants the same things in life—the pursuit of happiness, basic human rights, and freedom.

We must relinquish this feeling that we are separate and disconnected and bring back community and connection. The funny thing is, without the constant technology disruptions, being isolated and facing nature's vastness, I found that people were even more connected. Across the vastness of the ocean, despite not seeing another living soul for days on end, I have found more open hearts and willingness to help one another than I ever did when I lived in the big city. In contrast, after two years in a high-rise with hundreds of apartments, I did not even know one neighbor by name.

The invisible barriers we put between each other only serve to protect our sensitive egos—they do not foster our growth as human beings. We judge. I've judged. Now, the moment I catch myself, I stop and practice compassion. I'll extend a warm greeting whether I see a long-haired sailor on a raggedy-looking boat or a well-groomed yachtie-looking captain on a powerboat. Experiencing the diversity of boaters across sailing communities who strike up unlikely friendships no matter what their backgrounds, helped me stop stereotyping. Judgments aren't real, they are the programs and limiting beliefs playing in our heads. We are not that different. I've met too many people in bathing suits and flip-flops to know that underneath it all; we're all the same.

What separates us is fluff. Filters are created by culture, beliefs, politics, past experiences, and background. Filters disappear when the fragility of life is suddenly present. If I had let those dictate who I interacted with or avoided, I would have missed out on so many people who colored my kaleidoscope!

The people and their stories are simply too good to keep to myself...

We met the globetrotting Aussie who circumnavigated twice around the globe. On his second turn, he had been so long at sea that he chickened out and came into port when he reached the shores of Australia. He wanted to keep going but his girlfriend at the time freaked out and demanded he dock. He pulled in, did not tie a line but got close enough to the pier so that she could jump off the boat with her belongings as he sailed right back out. We met over 8,000 nautical miles later in an anchorage and listened to his hilarious stories told with the thickest accent. What a colorful night filled with laughter.

Then there were the retirees, two out-of-shape landlubbers who recently sold their bed & breakfast to move aboard full-time. A bit older than most cruisers; one needed to have a knee replacement and the other had flexibility issues. With zero nautical, mechanical, or electrical knowledge, we worried about them for the longest time but later learned that a decade later they were still roaming the islands.

How about the clean-cut sporty couple whose boat was in the most impeccable shape. Everything was rebuilt or brand new, despite being an older sailboat. Hardworking and very knowledgeable, they were always doing a boat project. They mostly stayed away from the cocktail hour crowd and looked a bit uppity but when we got to know them we became fast friends. We'd go devoure buckets of fresh clams and home fries at a little-known local hangout.

Of course you've seen examples of, "the old salt." This is the rough, thick-skinned sailor with a constant days-old beard, yellow teeth, cigarette hanging in the corner of his mouth, short, stocky, and always sweaty. We met an old salt who was absolutely in love with his tall new wife—she had recently moved aboard his craft and was trying to adapt to the lifestyle. His mouth was as colorful as his shirts. Their boat needed work, yet, every chance he got, he sailed away with broken stuff. That landed him in trouble, stranding him at sea where he had to be hauled back a few times by Sea-Tow. He knew how to hack and patch everything on boats but just never seemed to get around to actually fixing it.

Oh, and there was the life-loving, French-only-speaking, Frenchman and his bride. Millionaires from selling hair accessories and traveling the world on their medium-size, very average motorboat. She in adorable French fashion and he in polo shirts and loafers. The laughs we had with these two circled around comparing sport boats and sailboats and our French from Canada versus their French from France. We stayed in contact and met up over the years. Their smiles and eagerness to explore other countries and make connections, despite the language barrier, were absolutely contagious.

We also met and became very dear friends with 'the boat that never moves' folks. These were boat-savvy individuals who fixed everyone's boat but their own. The constant, unmistakable aroma of cannabis welcomes you every time you slide down the companionway. With barely any space to move aboard, there is always room for rescue dogs and dog sitting for anyone going out of town. The biggest hearts don't need room (and apparently don't need to roam).

There was the sport fisherwoman who traveled to every contest and game fishing tournament, as fast as she could, and fished for hours on end. She had short bobby blond hair tucked underneath a baseball cap and a pretty suntanned face. She wore long-sleeved sun wear and white sunblock on her lips and nose. Always in beige board shorts, her long legs were tanned and her feet sported the priciest boat shoes recommended for the best grip so as not to slip when she's fighting the big ones. She lives for the next catch, the best lures, the best tips, and spends her time fishing, teaching other women how to fish, making lures, and getting her boat ship-shape for her next run.

Another notable character was the single lawyer on the tiny sailboat defending our rights—as well-informed as an encyclopedia, yet humble and kind.

Then, there was the couple who reminded me of my parents. They introduced us to Irish chicken pot pies, taught Eric how to make Ceasar salad dressing from scratch, and drove on the wrong side of the road (with a steering wheel on the right side). Older than us by almost a generation, they built their boat and sailed it south from Canada and decided to live aboard and retire where winter wouldn't reach them. She volunteered her teaching services to local schools on the islands. He was a retired pilot with the kindest smile, delightful accent, and a knack for engineering.

And there were two of my girlfriends, both sail boaters, each on different sides of the political aisle. One left the marina on her bicycle to canvas the beaches and register voters for the next election, the other disputed her concerns with unequivocal passion. One, a cat lover who taught her cat to potty in the toilet onboard (seriously!), and the other shared her boat with two large furry dogs. Both adventurers and powerful women in their own spheres. Both are funny as hell and able to talk and defend their views for hours on end. Both love to help others and would never pass up a chance to support their friends, even making a career out of it. Both love the lifestyle they chose and their families.

The list goes on and on…

The richness of life lies in our connections.

We've bartered boat parts, traded books, and exchanged advice and recipes floating in the middle of nowhere. We've answered Mayday calls, towed strangers, and received help countless times. We've had our dinghy rescued by strangers and appreciated joint efforts from a bunch of unknown boaters to get us off a sandbank.

We've tried exotic foods, listened to foreign music, and learned about other cultures. We've made friends from all over the world. It's now easy for me to connect with people from all walks of life, and I'll never feel small again because someone is wearing a Gucci suit or driving an expensive car. I just picture them in flip-flops and know that sand in their butt crack bothers them as much as it bothers me.

LESSON: Align compassion with humanity

Our compassion, love, and forgiveness live in our fourth chakra, the heart chakra. It is located in the middle of our chest, the *heart center*. When our heart chakra is balanced we experience self-love, compassion, and love for others.

By being kind to every living thing and letting go of judgments toward others, you activate and balance this important chakra.

What would be your first thought seeing a long-haired, suntanned, tattooed, slightly disheveled leather-faced man walking on the beach? BUZZER! You would probably deduce that he is a bum, and walk away, afraid he may beg for money, or be dangerous. What would shift inside you if you expanded your realm of possibilities? See how it feels when you conclude that he is a decorated retired veteran sailing around the world—stopping in every port to bring help and supplies to small communities in need.

If we are to survive on this planet, our compassion cannot be selective. We need to extend it to every human being. We have become accustomed to judging everyone for everything all the time. On the harshest scale, we judge appearance, culture, spiritual beliefs, sexual orientation, and country of birth. But we also judge people for subtle things like accent, their life choices, what vehicle/boat they buy, their level of education, what food they bring to a potluck, even the type of yoga they practice! The list is never-ending and I'm guilty of it too.

When I catch myself being judgmental, I stop to observe my inner chatter. I replace it with compassionate words—reminding myself that we are all perfectly imperfect humans—and then I let it go. I forgive myself for allowing my beliefs-fears-unkind behaviors to cloud my perspective and open myself to a new outlook that is kind and inclusive.

When I align myself with compassion, I am guided by my heart and intuition, and then my actions reflect a deeper trust in life—unhindered by my ego mind.

I've been judged harshly in the past, and it hurts. I learned to brush it off and cut people off to avoid the pain. But this only creates barriers and more disconnect between you and the people in your life. When I am being judged, I choose to let go and focus on my truth. Knowing that others judge me because they see me through the distorted lens of their fears and beliefs, there is no need for me to react, and let it affect my day. It's hard sometimes, especially when it comes from a loved one. On occasion, I choose to have a talk with the person. Regardless, I love myself unconditionally and nothing anyone can say will change that fact.

Being a rebel will bring criticism. Living outside of society's pre-determined, approved choices of appropriate lifestyles and behaviors scares people. I mention this only to bring awareness. A deeply key concept to embed is that every-single-time we judge and condemn people's actions and decisions—it is based on our own fears and beliefs. In other words, it's not them, it's you.

When we first moved to Florida and bought a sailboat at a fairly young age, our decision was judged as frivolous and irresponsible by a lot of people. Moving aboard and having the dream of chartering and traveling the world sounded outrageous and was laughed at, and we were branded as immature hippies (yay!). Just moving to another country created a lot of waves, and some hurtful things were said by close family members. I now understand that the comments made were not about us, but rather about them. Simply put, everything out of the typical order of standard life is scary and makes people uncomfortable, and society tells us that it is to be avoided at all costs.

In time, of course, most have come to appreciate how seriously blessed our lives are, even if they still do not understand the choices we made. Fast forward twenty years, and now that we are slowly approaching retirement age—suddenly it is acceptable and even celebrated that we lived on a sailboat and realized our dream.

When did the switch happen? How does the passage of time make anything more or less acceptable? We are still the same couple. As we grow, we often regret some of the past things we judged harshly and change our stance to applaud the trailblazers. I say happy are the sailors, mountain climbers, scavengers, artists, philosophers, and deep-sea divers who roam this world far and wide, high, and low, and in the process, discover just how vast their psyche is, how limitless the courageous human heart is, and how brave and inspired their soul is. Thank you for coloring this world with your magic.

Being on the outskirts, being in life-changing situations, and questioning everything has pushed me to erase my limits and reinvent myself. I am forever grateful for my companion, who has sparked much of this deep sea/deep soul exploration. At my self-excavation site, I found unconditional love for myself and the human race.

QUESTION: In what ways do I judge others? ... myself?

 ACTION: Eye gazing

This exercise can be done with just about anyone in your life, including complete strangers (a real eye-opener—pun intended—with people you don't know). It is a meditative practice in Buddhism, Sufism, and Tantra. Eye gazing is also done in a lot of yoga and personal growth workshops for good reasons; it is one of the most powerful bonding exercises I've ever experienced. It has moved me to tears on many occasions, and I've always come out of this exercise feeling like I've found a long-lost brother or sister, regardless of whether they were friends or strangers before the exercise. There is something magical that happens when two people stare into each other's eyes without words and hold the gaze for a certain amount of time.

Barriers are broken, connections are made, and profound healing can happen. It may start as initial shyness, then move into acknowledging and seeing the other person for the human being that they are, and recognizing that we are reflections of each other, and the longer you gaze the more introspective the experience becomes, moving you into your own inner journey and how you and they become one. I've practiced gazing for up to 62 minutes with complete strangers, and it is profound and transformational.

The act of being seen, as you are, with no mask or chatter, generates respect, recognition, acceptance, and an immense sense of love.

Sit across from your partner facing each other, knee to knee. Place a timer by your side, and gaze uninterruptedly into each other's eyes, without talking, for 11 minutes. Do not break your gaze for any reason. Eye gazing deepens our relationship with others, and ourselves, and helps improve connection and communication.

9. Salty Goodbyes—Spirit Voyage

Align with the Divine

Beloved Hatch and Cappy, "Life is short, play hard."

"The sands of time forever slip through our fingers, but stardust lives forever." —Carole

In our early years aboard Windsong, Eric and I became fast friends with our neighbor Bob, an airline mechanic who lived on a houseboat just a few slips down from us. Best known for his wise-ass jokes and the most decadent garlic bread, Bob had the biggest heart, except if you did laundry on Wednesdays around 3:20 pm—his time slot. Nobody dared use the single washing machine at the marina or they found themselves in salty waters, and their clothes possibly suffered from it! You recognized his mischievous eyes when he was getting ready to pull a prank, and if you sat by him, you had better be quick-witted cause you were in for a ride. Mister Brown was a hard guy not to love, and you enjoyed every minute trying not to laugh.

Since Eric and I were greenhorns, we welcomed the advice of fellow boaters and Bob was always eager to help.

His floating home was a 47-foot 1956 Harbormaster called My Fair Lady. It had an upper and lower deck with a roomy interior and extra rooms downstairs, where my first dog loved to snooze.

Bob was part of the instigating crew behind my magazine, Real Sailors, and wrote a fan-favorite column under the pen name Riveratbob. Since Eric was often working when I had magazine-related events to attend, Bob became my sidekick and we scoured nautical festivals, gatherings, and boat races, raising hell wherever we went (thank you, Bob!). He's been there for us on many occasions, and we consider him our brother to this day.

So, when my brother-from-another-mother introduced me to his parents, not surprisingly, there was an instant connection. As lively and funny as Bob was and with more stories to tell, Cappy and Hatch were a hoot!

His elderly parents would regularly drive down from Daytona Beach to spend a few weeks on board. We'd share potluck dinners, go sailing, and spend hours listening to his father's World War II stories.

When it's not your time…

Cappy flew B17 bombers in the war. He got shot down over the English Channel and survived to tell the tale. He ended up in the cold waters in the dead of night, with only two surviving crewmembers. They were fortunate to get out of the crash alive, Cappy was uninjured, but one of his mates had a broken leg. If they didn't get out of the frigid waters within fifteen minutes, they would die from hypothermia. Cappy said he always thought he was a good swimmer until he saw this injured guy swim to safety.

They scrambled to reach a German buoy close by, swimming on adrenaline and the rush to hide and survive enemy bombers. They made it to the beacon grateful for the luck so far considering they'd just been shot out of the sky. They had to drag their mate up by the collar to lift him on the marker and sat completely exhausted but somewhat secure for now. At least, they wouldn't drown, but if they didn't get rescued quickly, they would die from exposure to this wet freezing environment. That's if they didn't get shot by German patrols first.

Chapter 9 — Align with the Divine

They waited for hours hiding from German boats scouring the sea searching for targets and survivors with their spotlights. Those were the longest hours he lived through and those were the toughest guys. "War was war," he said.

They were rescued by an English military boat sailing by waving their friendly flag. This was not their time to die. Cappy and his remaining crew were taken to England and then went on to continue fighting in the war on the mainland for weeks while the rest of the world marked them as missing in action. For a few months, his wife, Hatch, didn't know if he was alive or dead. Imagine living before smartphones, and instant news cycles. She finally received a letter from him—the type of coded letters all servicemen wrote before departure not to divulge whereabouts if intercepted by the enemy, that told of easy times at the pub visiting the countryside—but it let loved ones know their soldiers were alive and safe.

Hatch worked for a manufacturer in New York that built bombs. One day soon after, a woman she worked with came running toward her yelling. Hatch immediately held her breath, thinking, something bad happened to Cappy. The woman placed a magazine in her hands and pointed at the young airmen on the cover, "Look there's your husband!" He was pictured sitting on top of a mountain in Italy bandaging a man's head and fixing his head injury after getting blown up. The photo ended up on the front of the Saturday issue. The next time she got a hold of him she said, "Now Cappy, that was not very nice." Alluding to his letter claiming he was on a tourist venture.

Then at 83, Cappy was legally blind, almost deaf, had advanced cancer, and limited range of movement, but that didn't stop him from enjoying the heck out of life. They were high school sweethearts and a remarkable couple. They made everyone around them better for knowing them. I remember seeing them dance after Cappy had a remarkable acupuncture treatment from our friend Scott who came to treat him on Bob's houseboat. To see him lovingly hold his wife and have the energy to spin her around on the finger pier while the ocean breeze gently bobbed the boats on each side was a rare sight. They must have been quite the pair in their younger years! Hatch at 78 years young was leading her man so they didn't fall off the dock (because he was blind), and Cappy was dancing to the rhythm of his heart. It was mesmerizing to see these two souls twirl in the sunset, still very much in love almost seventy years after they had met. We knew we were witnessing a very special kind of love.

Cappy was an amazing storyteller, and we'd all hang on his every word enticing him always to tell more, "Another story, Cappy!" He reveled in the attention and we loved his captivating tales. Hatch would laugh and sip her once-a-day medicinal glass of cognac. Cappy would start cussing and Hatch would holler, "Hey, there are ladies present," pointing at me. He would grumble and swear and pardon himself while everyone laughed. I'd excuse him, "Don't worry, Cappy, I'm a sailor—and I talk like one too!" with a wink and chuckle.

Hatch was full of positive energy. I called her "my adoptive mom" as we had a very special connection. Despite the generation gap, I could talk to her about everything. She was a spitfire and a bundle of wisdom. When she was on board, she polished and shined every inch of My Fair Lady. She said it was good exercise. Her favorite saying, one that stayed with me was, "If you don't use it, you'll lose it!" encouraging daily exercise.

She would sit Cappy in front of a stanchion (the small pilings that hold the lifelines around the boat), give him a rag with some polish, and let him go to work. He needed assistance because at his age with his blindness and mobility, the last thing we needed was for him to take a swim. When he was done, she would help him get up and move to the next one, set him up, and go about cleaning the rest of the boat.

Chapter 9 — Align with the Divine

The police from the marine unit stationed at the marina would come by and say hi and chat up a storm—yelling at Bob for making his dad clean the boat and wondering if it was legal. "What are you doing to this poor old man?" And Bob would reply, "If he wants to eat, he needs to work." And his dad laughed.

When they went back home, Hatch sent me letters with cut-out inspirational posts, quotes from church, cards, and tokens she thought I would like, and I would reply and tell her about our days at the marina. I began to look forward to going to our post office box, just to see if I had received something from Bob's mom. (We docked in different places, so we used post office boxes to get and forward our mail to wherever we docked at the time.) Occasionally, we called each other just to stay in touch. She loved to hear the latest gossip about marina life. Thinking about this reminds me of how special it is to get a letter in the mail from someone you love. I wish people would send them more often.

One sunny Sunday, we took Bob and his parents sailing on Windsong. At the time, Cappy was 83 years young, and Hatch was an energetic 78. It was a huge challenge getting the less mobile blind man onboard and secured into the cockpit, but we made it. We breezed on out of Port, off we went, letting them feel the magic of sailing once again. It was a warm November day, and the seas weren't too bad—for people who see, have balance, AND can move easily.

The boys decided it was time for a Titanic moment for the veteran. They wanted to bring him on the bow of the boat to feel the exhilaration and force of a 15-ton boat under full sails, soaring over the water with the waves crashing under his feet.

Bob and Eric each grabbed one arm and decided that there was no day like today to give him this likely last chance to feel the incredible sense of flying on the bow of a sailing vessel. At first, they tried to go the typical route to port side out of the cockpit, but it was too difficult to walk three people, side by side, even with the gentle waves. So,

Eric had the idea of unzipping and rolling up the cockpit windows and having them crawl on the foredeck through the middle opening to reach the mast. They took their time and the three of them walking on hands and knees, helping this old champ feel his way to the bow. They stood on each side as Cappy sat his back against the mast and put his head up feeling the wind against his skin, singing in the sails, and feeling the rise and fall of Windsong. For a fraction of a moment, when the boat was at the top of the wave and the wind filled the sails, we were suspended in midair, and every cell in our bodies felt like lifting off into the air. We were flying.

It gave us an immense sense of gratitude and freedom—a Titanic, "I'm on top of the world!" moment—and his grin was priceless. Hatch looked on with a mischievous smile and sparkles in her eyes, "He's loving this." Cappy wore the perfect t-shirt for the day; "Life is short. Play hard."

On our sail back, we heard a distress call over the radio. It was close by, so we tacked the sails and turned the iron sails on full speed and went for a rescue. It made for a little action but by the time we got there, a powerboat was helping—of course—but it might have reminded Cappy of his younger years.

When it's your time...

I think this was the last time I saw Cappy. We lost him to cancer.

A few years later, Hatch passed away quietly, joining the love of her life in the afterlife. When Bob asked if we could spread their ashes out to sea, Eric and I accepted the great honor of taking them on their last sail. So, on a somber Saturday morning, we set sail with a few friends, family, and some very precious cargo.

Chapter 9 — Align with the Divine

We sailed out of Port Everglades and aimed straight east for about ten miles until we reached international waters. It was just fitting to give them their last farewell and release their ashes into the Gulf Stream current so that it would take them up the sailing routes that follow the trade winds.

The Gulf Stream is a river that runs through the ocean. From our Florida location, it travels north to Cape Hatteras in North Carolina where it veers east into deeper ocean waters. Sailors have used ocean currents and trade winds to travel since the beginning of time. From there, the North Atlantic Current splits into different "paths," the Norwegian Current travels to the west coast of Europe, and the Canary Current turns south following Africa's coast and moves southwest toward the Equator, known as the North Equatorial Current. Then back in the Caribbean islands sailing the Antilles Current and entering the Florida Gulf Stream again having gone around the great Loop Current.

Cappy and Hatch loved the ocean. One can imagine they would enjoy the journey of traveling together and following the current, returning on occasion to sail along the Florida coast to greet their son Bob. A great metaphor for the afterlife voyages they'd just started.

Our hearts were heavy with grief and the sail was solemn despite the bright sun and beautiful ocean. Windsong sang with its sail fluffed in the wind and we shared memories, laughs, stories, and tears. Bob, who had lost his brother and sister, was the eldest and last surviving member of his family. His cousin and a few friends joined us for the trip.

We were miles away from land with only the ocean as our witness. We knew from the pull on the boat that we had entered the Gulf Stream a while back. It was time. We stopped Windsong and set ourselves adrift in the northern current. Bob took out Cappy's and Hatch's ashes. Standing on the bow of Windsong, he gave a short and heartfelt eulogy, and we passed around a bottle of Hatch's favorite cognac. Crying and toasting to them, we raised our glasses as we watched Bob turn over the containers and release their contents to the sea. The ashes swirled and created spirals with each other, spinning so that they eventually became one right before entering the sea. The ocean calmed. The boat completely stopped rocking. There wasn't any noise, birds, or movement except for the boat's drift. It was an eerily wonderful thing to experience. All eyes were on Bob and the spiraling phenomenon, until, out of the corner of my eye I saw movement. Surprised, I turned to see the biggest and largest butterfly cruise toward us from out of nowhere. It flew past the cockpit, fluttered its wings in our direction, and flew right in the middle of us standing and sitting on the foredeck. Everyone froze in shock. There was no rational reason why a butterfly would be ten miles out to sea, flying gallantly and greeting us at exactly this time. This particular butterfly was huge and impossible to miss. It had the most beautiful dark colors. It fluttered gently as if it was in a garden kissing flowers, instead, it was out to sea kissing everyone's spirit. Bob almost dropped the bottle of cognac as it flew over to greet him, hovering slowly past everyone, it did a 360 around Bob, and then turned around and flew back the same way it came. We were stunned.

I had never seen a butterfly all these miles out to sea, and this one was so large and unique. And no, it could not have been hiding away on Windsong, it came out of the blue sky to our starboard side and returned, disappearing on the ocean's horizon.

Oh, Hatch, oh Cappy, how we loved thee.

We felt like we'd just experienced an episode of The Twilight Zone. Geographically speaking, we were sailing in the Bermuda Triangle at the time. It took a minute or two after the butterfly disappeared for someone to utter a sound and break the spell. Then all at once, everyone burst out, "Oh my God, was this real?" "Did anyone else see that?" "Did this just happen?" "Yes!" We exclaimed, "Wow!"

We experienced a mystical moment suspended in time. We were present to our fortune of experiencing such a rare occurrence and grateful to the Forces that made it happen. The instant the butterfly disappeared, it felt like the wind picked up again, and Windsong fell back into rhythm with the waves. Astonished, relieved, happy, and awed, to have just witnessed Cappy and Hatch's last dance and flight into spirit. Everyone asked for a second round of cognac.

It was the perfect farewell to two amazing souls and a flawless launch to their "afterlife" journey. They were together again, sailing above the clouds and dancing on the waves of heaven. They made sure we knew that all was well in their new world.

The return trip was filled with a much higher spirit. After all, it wasn't a salty goodbye the moment that butterfly announced, "Until we meet again."

LESSON: Align with the Divine

Hatch had a lot of faith in life and the afterlife. She knew how precious life was for Cappy having survived the war and having lost a son and a daughter.

It was an absolute privilege to know these two incredible souls. The immense grief I felt following Hatch's death was profound. I felt that since I had not known any of my grandmothers growing up, the Universe provided me with one, and just for a while I had a nana.

I didn't believe in much before meeting them. Never stopped to think about those things. But when she passed, I felt a deep loss. After witnessing the butterfly sea burial, I started talking to her and asking for more signs. It may sound silly for some but when you lose someone you love you reach for anything. So, the following day I jumped off Windsong, grabbed the leash, and took Dingo for a much-anticipated walk to the beach. I asked Hatch,

"If you're there, show me a sign." Right then and there, a dove flew in front of me and landed in a low-lying branch right beside another dove that had been waiting. I jumped because it flew so near me that it surprised me. We all stared at each other and I burst out crying. Oh my God, my beloved Hatch was telling me, "I'm okay, I'm here with Cappy and we are together and free at last!"

Let go of your fear of dying and surrender to the magic and mysteries of Life. Embrace every moment wholeheartedly, and with complete surrender. Love with your heart wide open. Play every chance you get. Dance the night away. Even blind, deaf, and sick—there is always something to be grateful for. Magic is real. Trust in what the eyes can't see. Prepare for the inevitable and make arrangements for an easy transition for your loved ones, but never let death cloud your living days. Trust in the Divine. Activate your seventh chakra located on the crown of your head by nurturing your spirituality.

QUESTION: I want to be remembered for…

 ACTION: Letter to the lost souls

Write a letter to someone who either passed away or with whom you've lost touch. Complete any unfinished business you have with them. Let them know how you feel, whether it is to ask for forgiveness, say you forgive them, thank them, or say your peace and tell them how they hurt you. Pour it all down on paper. Then burn the letter and feel a peaceful resolution as you watch the smoke evaporate. You can also write a letter to the Divine, or any higher power you believe in.

10. Resist the Elements—Dinghy Mishap

Align Decisions with Mindfulness

Carole and Sarah on Windsong.

"If you think you can achieve great things without taking action, think again."
—Carole

At this point, we weren't greenhorns, but we weren't mature sailors either. In hindsight, it was probably obvious to the old salts observing us from the dock, that what we were about to attempt would be good entertainment for anyone out of harm's way. "Hey Joe, check out this guy coming into the marina!"

We had precious cargo onboard. The kids were on board again—now twelve and fourteen—they had flown down from Canada for spring break, this time accompanied by their grandma. It was the first time the kids had a vacation with her. After Eric's divorce from his first wife, and our move to Florida, the kids had been in their mother's care and came to visit on holidays and vacation. Contact with their paternal grandparents was few and far between. It was a great opportunity for them to renew ties.

The kids had stayed onboard several times, but we had only taken my mother-in-law out once, on a day sail. She wasn't the sporty type and Eric was eager to show her the thrill of sailing without rocking her boat. She got the thrill all right, you'll have to ask her about her rock and rolling adventure!

The forecast for the last few days was disappointing; scattered thunderstorms, windy and gusting up to 25 knots with seas 6 to 9 feet and higher in the Gulf Stream. More of the same was expected for the next few days. We scratched our float plan to cross to the islands (unwilling to submit our greenhorns to these offshore conditions) and sailed south in coastal waters, dodging weather from anchorage to anchorage.

The partial clouds were sailing fast above us, threatening a downpour one minute and offering generous blue skies the next. Despite the occasional showers, the spring breakers enjoyed sun and fun—except for a drastic 25° degree temperature drop one night, which didn't scare the Canucks one bit but sent Floridians (including me) looking for our tuques and parkas. On our intimate 41-footer, we made it memorable with teasing, laughter, generational stories, and adventures. The mood was happy, despite the gusty wind remaining constant, but we could see our brood needed a break.

We sailed into Plantation Yacht Harbor in Islamorada to get out of the chop, rest, and refuel our crew's morale. It was blowing 25 to 30 knots.

Looking at the layout of the marina Eric said, "We're backing up."

There was an awful lot of wind to be doing this maneuver, but the captain was confident that he could spin the boat and back it into the slip. It was the usual way we docked, and he'd done it many times before in calmer weather. This approach allowed us to drop our plank from the stern onto the dock and simply walk on and off the boat. With finger piers that extend to the side of boats, we were too short to reach the opening in our side safety line (doorway), so we'd have to coax mother-in-law to do some acrobatics and jump over the bow rail onto the dock which was quite a few feet down. Then, to get back onboard, she'd have to rock-climb-style her way up by straddling the anchor, lifting herself up, then climbing over the bow rail, around the genoa sail and roller furling—all without injuring herself or falling in the water. It was

Chapter 10 — Align Decisions with Mindfulness

totally doable yet physically challenging for a mom-in-law who wasn't athletic, and also, unnecessarily dangerous.

A boat doesn't back up like a car. It's like trying to dance with Vaseline slippers on an icy road. The principles of propulsion on water, momentum, float, drift, and current are more dynamic than four tires gripping solid ground. Not counting that each boat and propeller have a particular direction they favor. Windsong had a right-hand prop, so it always swung to port in reverse.

We found our slip and Eric stopped the boat allowing the momentum to carry us into alignment. We were in the perfect position to reverse, a vertical T right across the slip that the dockmaster had radioed us to use for the night. We were towing our inflatable dinghy for the trip and had temporarily relocated it to the bow to give us room to maneuver. I prepped my lines around the boat and tied them in cleats, ready to be thrown. I stood on the bow, nervously waiting, spring line in hand ready to lasso a piling and secure our position once in the slip.

This was the critical moment. Safety and success depended on everything going perfectly. If we didn't master this crucial part of backing into the slip, it could spell disaster. It was like parallel parking a car except if we missed, we would crash into our surroundings and their vessels were worth hundreds of thousands more than our ride. It was tricky even without any wind.

With all tension and eyes on Eric, he shifted Windsong in reverse and spun the wheel to bring the stern (back of the boat) around and back into the slip. Then it happened.

We lost steering.

Rendered completely powerless, and unable to maneuver, we were at the mercy of the elements. Absolute panic set in as an untimely 30+ knots gust howled and captured us and pushed Windsong—now a 15-ton fiberglass moving missile—toward the neighboring boats at ramming speed. We had been navigating at a decent pace to counter the windy effect, so we weren't at our usual fair weather slow pace. Without a way to slow our momentum, or reverse, we were helpless to stop it.

We were going to crash on two large yachts sticking out beyond the pilings of their slip.

I cringed.

I saw dollar signs burning our pocketbook via insurance deductible and fees to pay for the damage we were about to potentially cause.

The dinghy had gotten loose.

Blown by the wind it drifted toward the back and its tow line sunk and fouled the propeller, seizing it, and stalling us just as we were about to maneuver into the slip. We were dead in the water. The wind was our enemy now.

The kids were obviously scared, and mother-in-law started crying. Oh crap. All were cautioned not to move and stay in the cockpit.

The prop had spun the line so tightly that the only thing keeping the dinghy afloat was its positive buoyancy. It was glued to our stern, its nose slightly diving down by the tightness of the line hooked below. At least now it would act as a massive bumper, helping us to fend off the back.

Expecting the bow to take the worst hit, Eric ran to the front and used all humanly possible force to push us off the neighboring trawler and soften the blow while I ran to the back and jumped off Windsong and into the dinghy which squeezed between us and a neighboring boat. I pushed with all my might against the hull of the other yacht to try to smooth our landing and avoid getting our dinghy crushed to pieces. I heard the inflatable screech under pressure as it squeezed so tightly. I expected to hear a big "Pow," but it didn't explode. Ouf.

Chapter 10 — Align Decisions with Mindfulness

We bounced off the boats a few times and Windsong finally settled and stopped.

I was on an adrenaline high and could feel my heartbeat through my clothes, drumming at 200 miles per minute.

Everyone was okay.

We had done minimal damage except a bit of a scratch on one of the swimming platforms.

I felt like melting down to hide, and like superwoman at the same time.

The marina staff and concerned boat owners watched and shouted advice. We had landed snuggly fit perpendicular to three slips and stuck out like a sore thumb.

We tied off so as not to drift any further, and placed bumpers to avoid causing any more damage. We paused to settle our nerves and regroup.

When sailing, wind was appreciated and necessary, but dreaded when docking, and an absolute enemy when drifting around expensive yachts at the mercy of the elements.

With the wind blowing hard against us, even with our overpowered 85hp Perkins Diesel on full throttle, it would not be sufficient to steer our bow off the pilings and into a 25 to 30 knots wind. There was no way this boat would move without assistance.

Eric sprang into action. He grabbed his knife, mask, and snorkel, and dove underwater to cut away the dinghy line and clear the prop.

Windsong instantly regained steerage and the tender was freed.

Once that was done, he brewed a plan and issued orders. We had a huge spool of hurricane anchor line that took the whole space between the ladder and bulkhead* in the aft cabin. 200 feet of pristine brand new 7/8" line that we'd been saving for hurricanes, or for just such emergencies.

> * A bulkhead is a boat wall that partitions the interior.

He grabbed the spool and threw it in the dinghy leaving me to comfort and prepare the crew while he ran across the channel. The marina had a large breakwater jetty that ran parallel to the entrance channel, and we were going to winch ourselves out of trouble.

He reached the other side, carefully hiking over rocks, and tied the line to the biggest tree he could find. Making his way back, he slowly unspooled the line, hopped in the dinghy, and carefully dinghied back letting out the line and bringing the bitter** end back onboard.

> **The bitter end of a rope is the loose unsecured end that you work with and fasten to the ship.

He tied it to the anchor windlass (the most powerful winch we have onboard) and started to forcefully move the bow into the wind. This was going to work. Windlass are made to haul hundreds of pounds of tackle—anchor and chain—and pull three times the weight of your boat. That little motor was a Hercules and chugged away at the line, moving our bow into the wind, and spitting out line on the other side. Once we were positioned straight onto the wind; we had less windage and would not get caught and slam back on the pilings.

We were ready. We would have to move very fast.

Eric ran to the helm after yielding his spot at the winch to his son whom we had gloved and prepped, and I stayed by his side. Sarah and Ginette stayed out of the way and kept a nervous lookout. The wind was still blowing 20 to 25 knots with gusts.

At the wheel, the captain put the motor in drive and steered forward while his son winched and I tailed the line behind him, making sure it didn't get caught back in the windlass and lock, or end up in the water in our prop again!

It worked; we were turning. With the combination of our 85hp Perkins diesel, winch power, and tying our bow across the jetty directly into the wind, we eased off the pilings and moved toward the center of the channel.

We cleared the boats and pilings!

Except that we were tied from the windlass to the tree. There wasn't anyone on the jetty to untie the tree so we had to let go of our end. I helped our young crew. We freed up the winch and grabbed about 100 feet of heavy bundled-up line that we pulled and winched, and lifted it up and passed it around our roller furling (holds the genoa sail to the bow of the boat), then cleared the line from our hanging anchor, and finally threw it overboard on the other side so we could sail away free from it. Phew!

And then, Murphy's Law struck—the line got tangled in the dinghy's prop and I had to jump in the dinghy again (damn this day) to let the line loose. Geez!

Free at last! A dockhand screamed over, "Don't try to back in the slip, just dock on the main pier down a few slips!"

With the thick line sinking behind us, we motored over to the main dock and had a perfect landing in front of the office; this was on a side dock instead of in a slip (they probably wanted to keep an eye out for us and didn't want a repeat fiasco).

We tied the boat, turned off the motor, Eric used the dinghy to go fetch his line, and that was the end of our plight. That's when my legs turned into a ragdoll, and I had to sit down. Who needs the gym?

Eric went to see the other boats and talked to the boat owners and dockmaster. Only one boat was scratched on its varnish. We took a picture for insurance purposes and gave him our business card, but the owner waved us off saying not to worry about it. Everyone was very kind.

This lesson cost us a little bit of pride but thankfully not a lot of green.

To this day, my captain still gets upset when he reminisces because he knows he would have been able to bring it in the slip if it hadn't been for that darn line. Just a few more feet and we would have been home free.

Sailing: 90% relaxation, and 10% sheer panic.

LESSON: Align decisions with mindfulness

You would think that one of the simplest things to know is when you are in alignment with your goal, but surprisingly it is not. I feel it's because we are too immersed in the situation and need emotional distance. We've all heard, "In hindsight, I would have ___*(fill in the blank)*___" because once it's in the past we are somewhat detached from the emotions, and our nerves have settled. When you're in it, tunnel vision might set in, and it takes either drama or trauma to make you realize that there is an easier way. The goal you seek may not be necessary at all. The resistance you meet is a sign.

I've faced resistance from so many things in my life and it used to aggravate the heck out of me. As a good Taurus, I would charge ahead and just say, "Ramming speed!" I now realize that resistance is either one of two things:

1. I am out of alignment and being asked to realign my mind's goals with my heart's purpose.
2. I am being redirected toward something better and more aligned with my best interest.

Being mindful is listening to that guiding hand trying to encourage you to be more authentic and aligned with yourself, and more aligned with your path.

Sometimes it comes as a little nudge—like your dinghy running out of gas on your way to an important meeting when you already felt it wouldn't be a good client for you. Other times it's a series of events that derail your day and make you pause and reassess—like running out of water in the shower, having to run naked through the boat (with shampoo dripping in your eyes) to switch to the auxiliary water tank, then splashing seawater on your outfit as you dinghy over with a sputtering motor, reaching the dock and cutting yourself on the barnacles. All this to show up late to a meeting with someone that makes you feel uncomfortable.

Be mindful of how you make your decisions.

QUESTION: Where do I feel the greatest resistance in my life? Where does the energy flow?

 ACTION: Open-eyed meditation

I have the utmost respect for the Brahma Kumaris World Spiritual Organization. They have over 8,000 centers in over 110 countries around the world, with teachers spreading their message of peace, and educating people on how to meditate and live a happy life, free of charge. I've been deeply touched by some of their teachers and the teachings of Raja Yoga. My favorite thing I learned is open-eyed meditation. Rather than learning to meditate with closed eyes which is beneficial but hardly represents what happens when you are living your life in constant movement and interacting with others.

Simply choose a point of focus in front of you, and keep your eyes fixed on this point, as you observe your mind, and breathe deeply. When your mind wanders, simply refocus, and bring your awareness back to your focus point. Practice this for 3 minutes a day for a week, then work up to 10-15 minutes and more.

Learning to master your mind while your eyes are open and distractions are around you, teaches you to stay centered, present, and connected with your essence despite the drama that is happening around you. You will develop awareness and mindfulness and be able to stay calm and connected even in the diciest of situations!

11. Magic Underway—A Reiki Sail

Align your Chakras

Two of my dearest friends, Belinda (left), and Kim (rigth) on our girl weekend.

> *"The deeper in nature, the closer to spirit."*
> —*Carole*

A group of girlfriends and I used to gather in the Keys once a year for a weekend of sisterhood magic. Tight-knit, some of us had known each other for decades, while a few were fairly newcomers. We'd been at each other's weddings, celebrated births, cried on each other's shoulders, and were growing from a rowdy bunch of ex-bikers, ex-pats, some ex-cowgirls to new spiritual enthusiasts.

We all felt to some degree that we had outgrown part of our lives and explored ways to feel more aligned. These mini-retreats gave us an opportunity to connect on a deep level, discover parts of ourselves we didn't even know existed, and dabble in the arts of mysticism.

One of the newcomers in the group was my first Reiki teacher. She introduced us to an enchanted world of tarot cards, energy healing, divinations, and all kinds of ceremonial practices that were enticing but foreign to us.

I wanted this retreat to be extra special and some of my girlfriends just loved coming aboard while others had never sailed and were eager to try. So, Eric and I decided to sail Windsong 90 miles south so we could take them sailing, snorkeling, and enjoy on-the-water activities on our special weekend.

[Screeching sound]

Wait. What? Didn't I say, "A weekend of *sisterhood* magic?"

If you're wondering why my husband was part of this intimate group of women, well, he was named "honorary girlfriend" for the weekend to the dismay of the group's other spouses. He had to undergo an embarrassing initiation where we made him wear bras on top of his head, stretched over his ears and strapped under his armpits, and swear an oath that he would not divulge anything about what he heard or saw that weekend. We took compromising pictures as blackmail material to curb any inkling he would have of breaking our confidence and spilling our secrets. Seriously, it was all done in good fun and sealed with a rum and cheers!

My girlfriends love talking with Eric about the "BIG" questions in life. He has the ability to connect and listen—when he wants to—on a very deep level. I've woken up a few times in the middle of the night to find the bunk empty and Eric at the marina picnic table talking with my girlfriends about the meaning of life, if there was a God, and life after death. Not being a big sports fan, he'd often be found hanging with the girls in the kitchen instead of watching the Superbowl. He was a confidant to a lot of my soul-sisters, often making Eric and I the go-to couple when someone was having trouble or needed advice.

Thus, it only felt right that he be allowed to join our little gathering, so we sailed down for the occasion and spent the weekend anchored by the oceanfront resort where my girlfriends stayed.

Lucky for us, our good friend Bobby owned the watersport company on the hotel grounds and helped the girls get a good deal on the rooms. This place had a killer view of the ocean, white sandy beaches, flowers, palm and coconut trees everywhere, hammocks and long chairs strategically placed around the grounds, two pools, a Jacuzzi, a tennis court, an outdoor bar, and of course our favorite hangout spot, Bobby's

Chapter 11 — Align your Chakras

Tiki Hut. Decorated with a welcoming pineapple flag (means welcome in Hawaii), cozy chairs, and ocean treasures, you could rent all the water toys you could imagine; Hobe Cats (small catamaran sailboat), paddle boats, kayaks, snorkels, etc.

Smaller boats sailed into a lagoon that housed a few local sportfishing boats, with floating docks for visiting skiffs. Dolphins or manatees occasionally swam in, and fishermen fed the pelicans every afternoon as they cleaned the day's catch. Right beside it was a two-story opened tiki hut that felt like a huge tree house—this is where we did our morning yoga. The incredible view extended for miles on the horizon, and we pinched each other at how fortunate we were.

Only approximately 250 miles southeast, Cuban immigrants dreamt of escape. Recently a tiny, red-painted, wooden boat barely larger than a canoe with 20 desperate souls had landed on this beach to seek a better life. It now served as a decoration and reminder not to take anything for granted.

Left to the northeast side, you saw Whale Harbor Channel, the island inlet that crossed from the Atlantic Ocean to the bay on the side of the Gulf of Mexico, and on the side of the channel, the famous Islamorada Flats where locals and tourists gathered every day to frolic in the shallow water and cool off.

It was an idyllic place for our getaway.

Windsong was anchored on the ocean only 50 feet from the beach, in the tiniest natural lagoon surrounded by dangerously shallow banks. It was treacherous for a boat our size to anchor there so our buddy guided us in with his skiff, veering left and right following an intricate underwater channel to reach the protected pool. Sailboats rarely (if ever) anchored there.

Girls' weekends didn't get much better than this.

We channeled our yaya-sisterhood and called to the moon, danced barefoot in the sand till late in the night, poured our hearts out to each other, explored, and dinghied everywhere we could, snorkeled the reef, splashed the flats hiding under straw hats floating for hours until our skin shriveled up. For many of my girlfriends, it was a rare getaway from a hectic city life filled with kids, commitments, and work. Here we could drop the façade, let it all go, and simply be ourselves. Free to rant, cry, celebrate, and be sisters to each other.

The weekend became a never-ending soul-quenching reggae song. But the party was over. Everyone was sunburned, exhausted, some hungover, all feeling a bit of a toll from the non-stop festivities.

It was Monday and Eric and I had to sail Windsong back to its current berth in Dania Beach, although only a few hours' drive by car, it would take us approximately 8 hours by sea.

Four of my girlfriends decided to sail back up with us. It was the perfect time to initiate the non-sailors and show everyone why I loved Windsong so much.

We stowed their luggage below and packed enough snacks and beverages for the day-trip to feed an army. Their nervous excitement filled the air, and it was great to have so many dear friends onboard. Since it's usually only Eric and me on the boat, the giggling busy-bodies were a welcomed presence.

After a crash course on safety and emergency measures, we got underway.

Once we got into Hawk's Channel, we settled into a rhythm with the rocking boat and the waves. It was almost trancelike after a weekend feeling spent. Everyone looked blissfully happy and tickled to end our special gathering with a sailing adventure.

Chapter 11 — Align your Chakras

One of our sisters, Kim, had confided in us over the weekend that she was recently diagnosed with large kidney stones. She had been in a lot of pain and wasn't feeling good. She was able to pass one with medication, but the doctor told her that the second one was too large, and located in an area where it could not pass naturally. She would have to undergo laser surgery to break it up. Kim was a nurse and knew what that meant. There were always risks in procedures, and it took a toll on the body. With two kids at home and a busy life, she wasn't looking forward to the downtime or the intrusion into her body.

She was lying down on the bow of the boat admiring the huge white sails against the blue sky, completely enamored by the lifestyle, grateful for the weekend escape, yet contemplating the reality of what awaited her back in town. She was feeling the weight of this post-party reality check.

We had all taken our Reiki* level 1 and 2 classes together and asked Kim if we could do a Reiki circle around her. She was tickled and grateful.

> * Reiki is a Japanese energy healing technique where practitioners channel "universal energy" (qi, Chi) through the palms of their hands to the patient, to encourage emotional or physical healing. This type of alternative medicine is now accepted and practiced in well-known modern Western Hospitals.

We formed a circle around her between the foremast and cockpit and found ways to sit comfortably while nudging ourselves to hold on against the rocking of the boat. We invoked the Reiki energy and placed our hands over her. I had never done a session while underway on a boat, it felt exceptionally powerful. We were sailing at about six knots, the seas were smooth, but we were still sailing, following the rhythm of the waves. A smooth and easy mood, languorous even amorous, was created by the perfect pitch and poll, tension and release between the boat and the sea. The sound was amazing; the splashing of the bow in the water, the sound of the boat cutting through the elements, and of course the constant song of the wind. The sun was shining bright, but we were cool in the shade of the canvas.

We felt deeply connected in this moment. With each other, Kim, and the forces of nature all around us. We were flooded with life force and channeled it toward our dear sister, however she may need it. While we were in deep meditation, she was in a bubble of love. Her sisters were holding space for her, sending healing energy, and balancing her chakras. The boat was bustling with energy, and hopefully, her kidneys felt it, too.

Captain Fontaine was at the helm, unsure about what he liked to call, "voodoo magic" going on, but he respectfully turned the music down and let us do our thing.

Reiki sessions are different for everyone, but it's always a comforting and healing experience. Kim felt extreme heat and was overwhelmed with feelings of love and support, and her pain subsided.

After a while, we felt the energy settle, and a soothing sense enveloped everyone. We hugged silently, and slowly the circle dissipated, everyone going their separate ways, lost in their own world, connected with nature, the ocean, the boat, and the unseen realm that surrounds us. Immersed in silence and appreciation for what we were experiencing, the voyage home was a remarkably soothing sail.

Ten days later, Kim went in for her pre-op tests. She called me giddy with excitement: the kidney stone was gone. The doctor said it was impossible that she had passed it naturally, it was too large. And if it had miraculously broken into pieces, she would have felt it because it would have been extremely painful. He didn't understand what happened. It was a miracle.

No doctor—it was the power of Reiki. Kim never had surgery, and her stones never returned.

LESSON: Align your chakras

The first time that I discovered I could "feel" my energy was in my first Reiki level 1 class. I was floored. How could I have not known or felt this before?

Self-reiki is like taking an energetic cleansing shower. When I feel upset, anxious, or frazzled, or undergo any type of trauma, I do a self-Reiki healing session. It quickly grounds and recenters me and calms my energetic centers. Breath plays an important part. With the combination of focus, meditation, and energetic balancing it should—in my opinion—be taught to every individual on earth. I have not found anything that works so beautifully on me. I'm a fan for life.

On my healing journey, I explored many alternative healing modalities and learned to trust what I can't see. The health of my energetic body is as important as my physical body. In fact, oftentimes, dis-ease starts from an energetic blockage or stagnant energy.

Learning how to detect which of my chakras were out of balance and ways to unblock or regulate them was empowering. I protected my body from harm and protected myself from people who zapped my energy (energy vampires), so, why not protect my energy centers and add beneficial practices to my self-care routine? It heightened my awareness and helped me discover what my body needed to heal. Plus, it made me realize how connected we all are with this universal life force within and around us.

We have seven chakras, eight if you include our aura. Familiarize yourself with each and what energies they regulate so that you can target specific ailments and challenges in your life. I am including a chakra chart at the end of this book to help in your search.

QUESTION: Name 10 things you believe in that you cannot see:

 ACTION: Try Reiki

I have been practicing and teaching the Reiki Usui Shiki Ryoho method for years. I love it so much that I took my certification twice and joined several circles in the towns I traveled to. It has brought great comfort and healing into my life. For a while, I volunteered in a weekly healing circle for caregivers at Memorial Hospital. It was a great way to strengthen my connection, give back, and get over my shyness about sharing Reiki with strangers.

I initially took Reiki 1 & 2 in hopes of healing my capricious body. It was one of the first holistic wellness courses I took, and no matter what ails me, Reiki helps. I believe in it so much that I feel that Reiki Level 1 certification should be taught in high school. This is why my recommendation to you is to sign up for a class in your area.

Gentle yet powerful, it's available in almost every town across the country. Studies found that Reiki is effective in reducing pain, depression, and anxiety, boosting self-esteem and a positive outlook on life, and helping manage chronic health conditions. [4] Johns Hopkins, The Mayo Clinic, and the Cleveland Clinic are just some of the nation's top hospitals that offer Reiki in the areas of pain control and cancer complementary care alternatives. Where Western and Eastern medicine meet, we get a modern medicine that recognizes the body is an energetic system, therefore, bringing the body into a state of homeostasis and well-being becomes the focus of every doctor/patient visit.

Chapter 11 — Align your Chakras

At the very least, go to a Reiki circle or try a private session. Not only will it help you familiarize yourself with your body's energy, but the more you connect with Reiki, the more you can practice preventative energy management and support yourself in times of physical or emotional stress. Reiki supports the body, mind, and spirit, and helps you connect and balance all your chakras.

It's my go-to for settling nerves and getting rid of anxiety. When I can't sleep, or wake up in the middle of the night, I do a self-healing session, and within minutes I am back in la-la land. It can be done anywhere, anytime.

If you're in my area, I'd love to teach you!

12. An Empty Rum Barrel—A Pirate on the Ratlines

Align Boundaries and Respect

"Give a wide berth to loose cannon." —Carole

"Hey Carole…Carole, WAKE UP!" The voice said urgently.

"Whaaaaaat?" I crankily opened one eye to see Bobby, our good friend and overnight guest, crouching in the companion way trying to get my attention from the cockpit.

"I'm not sure about the boat rules, but Fontaine is up on the ratlines, waving a sword, halfway up the mast, and screaming at the neighbor!"

"Urgh. I lifted my head and peeked over his shoulder to see my husband's shadow up in the air. I screamed at the top of my lungs, "HONEYYYYY!"

"Yes?" He replied, pausing his mayhem.

"BE CAREFUL" I said, dropping my head on the pillow, and going back to sleep after seeing my friend's dumbfounded face.

The late-night noise level and music were deafening but I was adamant about getting some rest, exhausted from the day's festivities.

We had hoisted the Jolly Roger, it was regatta time and I was off babysitting duty.

Once a year, Key Biscayne is the scene for the most anticipated events in the Miami boating scene, The Columbus Day Regatta Races, and the Columbus Day Weekend at Elliot Key. What started over 60 years ago as a sailboat race to commemorate the October 1492 arrival of Christopher Columbus in the New World, grew to attract thousands of boaters who spend the weekend at anchor, some oblivious to the race taking place.

Although the racing event may have between 50 to a 100+ racing boats (depending on the year) and hundreds of spectators, the infamous on-the-water weekend-long party is the main attraction for most participants.

It's a ginormous boat rafting extravaganza with attendees by the thousands. Yes, thousands! Imagine the sight, from a deserted anchorage to a sea of boats of all shapes and sizes, sailing in to anchor and raft up for the weekend within a 1/2-mile radius!

It's absolute mayhem.

Stay far, far away if you don't want to get soaked by the biggest water guns you've ever seen, or if you expect a classy, quiet weekend at anchor, or if you are prudish at the sight of skin. Your ears will curl, and your eyes will squirm.

It's like a frat party for adults. A profusely disgusting number of adult beverages are served—giving everyone an excuse to let go of their inhibitions. The tardier it gets the more nudity abounds. This is not a family event.

Loud music blares every which way, Britney Spears, The Offsprings, Zeppelin, Bob Marley each boat trying to out-sound the other. The sportfishing boats had light shows and rows of six foot nightclub speakers tied to the top of their tuna towers, with dancers showing off their pole dancing prowess. There's always a rowdy redneck barge somewhere with tiki lights and sexy Daisy Dukes dancing to country music. Also, rafts with metal heads who can't hear themselves for the whole weekend. And, closing the ranks on the outskirts were the mega yachts, too big to anchor in the shallow flats, floating with eyes glued to their binoculars.

All types, tastes, and floats, voyeurs and participants descend from every corner (some even fly in) and cross the bay on pretty much anything that floats.

The main activity of the weekend is sightseeing in your dinghy. By sights, I mean looking for potential victims to soak. Many people, armed to the max with the biggest water gun they own, would bring buckets and hoses too. Temps are typically in the upper eighties; a drenching cool down is welcomed.

So, once we anchored, we grabbed a bunch of friends and went for a "run." We loved roaming the boat-made corridors and pick "fights" with other water rebels. Anyone armed was fair game. Sometimes we slipped and hosed down innocent bystanders. We were sure these folks would be better prepared the following year! Hee Hee Hee.

Over the years our water guns kept getting bigger and we got more stealth with our attack moves. Our favorite tactic was to go by a raft and exchange friendly water with them, letting them think they got us bad, then duck, circle around the neighboring raft, reload every water gun to their full potential, rev up the motor, and sneak attack them from behind, hammering them while they were still reloading. Now, that was fun! (Weren't we childish?)

Stealth maneuvers and attack strategies wouldn't save you unless you had a fast motor to get out of drenching situations. Once you were out of ammo, if you couldn't get away and your adversary still had the capacity to hose you down, you were using buckets to bail out the dinghy.

Goggles were helpful; many sunglasses succumbed to high water pressure and were lost at sea. But if anyone went around wearing a dive mask, they advertised themselves as looking for trouble.

Loading your water gun with illegal cold water from the cooler was highly disruptive and started quite a few salty wars. It was all done in good fun, and if you couldn't take a joke, this wasn't your place.

Baring your breasts would win you a great number of colorful beads, and some who grew tired of flashing simply discarded their tops and went about the weekend bare-breasted. Others (men and women), simply spent the whole weekend in their birthday suit. They of course had to sunscreen every part of their body!

It was an eye-opener for certain and might have even shocked some.

It was a rowdy, sexy, drunken galore; an on-the-water Mardi Gras with some in colorful costumes, and others in body paint.

Traffic "downtown"—in the center of the packed anchorage—got awfully tight, and we had to turn the motor off, get the prop out of the water, and row carefully through the sea swimmers, trying to not harm anyone. Partygoers hung out on blown-up pool floats of all shapes and sizes, noodles, and boat cushions and they kamikazed off boats splashing everywhere.

Some folks helped us by pushing our boat through as they swam away. We squeezed through small channels between boats with human obstacles afloat everywhere. We avoided colliding with deluxe floating coolers—complete with palm tree umbrellas and drink holders for the professional sunbathers.

Meanwhile, we were getting drenched from above and below (swimmers also hid guns underwater). We were trying to see where we were going but oftentimes ended up stuck in a cul-de-sac and had to

Chapter 12 — Align Boundaries and Respect

retrace our steps. Our captain had to be vigilant to venture downtown. A dinghy ride meant you had to prepare to be soaked to the bones.

Some people at the regatta took exhibitionism to the extreme; we witnessed a few R-rated scenes. Like the time we saw three couples dancing naked on the back of a Sea-Ray doing the conga line. Women and men were sandwiched between each other, swinging one way then swinging the other way—and they weren't holding each other by their hands if you know what I mean. It didn't take but a few songs as their prelude. They all disappeared down to the lower level and anyone could clearly suspect what happened below! We couldn't believe our eyes—in plain daylight.

I dare say, it was the most hedonistic party one could legally attend in the US (that I knew of, anyway).

Our rafts were much tamer. Yes, we acted like teenagers, drank, and were merry, but without the improper hanky panky. Our fun was simply to raft all our boating friends together and share great food, laugh like crazy, and play pranks on each other.

When we started going, so many boats tied themselves together that it grew into a ginormous floating island of boats, where we couldn't access the center of the raft "downtown" by water in any navigable way for a few days. It was impossible for a boat in the middle to leave before the party ended, no matter what the emergency, and this ended up causing security concerns.

Special measures were taken by law enforcement to minimize accidents, as they were overwhelmed by the amount of people who showed up uninhibited (some unhinged). Laws were put in place to tame and monitor the crowds.

- No more than five boats could be tied together. If you had more than 5 friends coming with boats, they'd start another raft and used the dinghy to visit.

- A minimum of 100 feet was the required distance between each raft (a group of boats tied together) so you had hundreds of "raft-islands" of 5 boats with people partying for the weekend.
- Boaters were urged to have a designated driver. BUI were as expensive (and dangerous) as a DUI.
- Boating safety requirements and spot checks were made so you had to carry the vessel's registration, a life vest for each passenger, sound device, etc., and had to be careful not to exceed passenger limits!
- Nighttime dinghying was highly discouraged, if you did, you risked ending up in the floating jail that law enforcement had temporarily set up on an anchored barge. Local law enforcement hired extra officers just for the weekend to help patrol the waters and hand out tickets. A friend of ours once spent the night there. It wasn't the raft party he was expecting!

Thus, when Bobby woke me up late in the second night of the Regatta, concerned about my husband being up by the mast hollering at the neighbor and waving a sword, I wasn't too concerned. He was in pirate-regatta mode. Eric had always taken partying to the extremes for as long as I had known him and this was his weekend to let the devil out (not that he needed an excuse). Frankly, I was sunburned and exhausted from splashing around all day, and honestly didn't care.

Later, I found out that the neighbor rafting next to us had put two anchors down when they arrived so when the tide changed in the middle of the night and hundreds of boats all swung the other way in unison, this fool didn't move an inch. What happens when one unit that is part of a formation doesn't follow the flow? It crashes into everything around it and creates pandemonium. Every single vessel in the bay that had been pointing east was now synchronously swinging to point west where the incoming tide was favoring. That meant that every 5-boat raft within 100 feet of this guy was slowly drifting toward the boats on his raft. And the ones around those would hit them in return. This created a big nautical knot of tied up boats (pun intended).

Just because someone is at a regatta, doesn't mean they have any common sense. The guy dismissed his neighbors, not budging an inch and they all waved at each other trying to figure out how to make him change his mind to fend off crashing into each other. This was all happening at night, when people were anchored for the night, inebriated and some frustrated, with tempers flaring.

After Eric tried to talk, or, actually scream some sense into him, attempting to be heard over the distance and music (the guy had turned off his VHF radio). Eric was waving and asking him to raise his second anchor to let the tide swing them like everyone on the bay. Eric grabbed his sword—yes, we carried a real sword onboard, a gift from a friend—he climbed up the ratlines* waving and screaming with all his might that if he didn't move his anchor, he would make him do so. When my man let his hair down, he looked like a crazy Viking (he had wild, long hair back then). His penchant for drama might have been a tad overly excessive, although I did find the waving of the sword up the mast (to make a point) hilariously funny.

> * Ratlines are lines tied between the shrouds that form a ladder used to go up to stow sails, perform rigging repair or be a lookout.

Shortly thereafter, that 5-boat raft ended up settling into synchronous flow with the rest of the crowd. Was it divine intervention? A change of heart? A sharp sword? Who's to say. What happened at the regatta stayed at the regatta!

The duel settled, we heard relief and gratefulness from other concerned boaters applauding the sudden joining to the flock. Every captain in the vicinity could rest knowing their boats were secure and they had avoided possibly thousands of dollars in damage, headaches, and heated arguments.

Throughout the weekend we had a never-ending show of friends and acquaintances sail by and say hi, welcoming everyone to hang out. We shared potlucks and squeezed everyone in at the table of the largest boat of the raft—always having extras for surprise visitors. I loved having my salty girlfriends around to talk about things only other sailors could understand. Yes, women talk heads, galley, inverters, storage, gimbal stove, and exchange liveaboard tips.

The men played pranks on each other, talked mechanic, and told racy jokes and tall tales. If we lucked out someone took out their guitars and played some tunes. Otherwise, we drained the battery bank playing music all night and plugged into the generators on the bigger boats to recharge.

We always anchored close enough to see the action, but far enough that we would not get drowned by the downtown music which played till the wee hours of the morning.

It was a "wet & wild" weekend of sunning our buns as well as an opportunity to hang out and cookout with our salty friends. Some people meet on camping trips and let out their crazy in the forest, we did it rafting on the water.

A fun activity was spending that Monday morning after with the remaining skeleton crew snorkeling and scouring the sandy bottom of the "downtown" area for whatever was lost overboard in the festivities. We collected a lot of trash but also found lost valuables like fancy jewelry, expensive sunglasses, a full stainless steel marine barbeque, and anchors. A great treasure hunt indeed—especially when we found money!

The regattas were a very fun time in our lives, but after some years, the treasure hunt became the highlight of my weekend and I knew it was time to chart a new course.

LESSON: Align boundaries and respect

We're all free to express and enjoy life any way we choose, as long as it doesn't hurt anyone (including ourselves). That includes our spouse—who we may not always agree with—if we want that same respect reciprocated.

When someone infringes on our boundaries and a crash is imminent, it makes us feel out of control and sends a warning bell. If we live in society, we must accept that we are part of a flock, and our actions affect others. Our freedoms must not infringe on other people's space. We must balance respecting others and enforcing healthy personal boundaries—even with our loved ones.

Learn to develop enough self-awareness to remove yourself from situations when your ways disrespect others. Otherwise, you might find a pirate ready to board your ship and remind you!

QUESTION: When, where, or how do I compromise myself?

ACTION: Radar warning: This does not belong to me

Imagine that you are the center of a radar screen. The circle closest to you includes your family, another one around them includes your friends, encircled by a larger one with all the people you know, and on the outskirts are strangers. The closer the circle, the more difficult it is to distinguish when drama targets us personally or our empathy.

It's easy to jump into our loved ones' troubles and make them our own because we love them and want to help. This cannot be done to the detriment of our inner peace. Adding emotional distance helps keep our minds clear and improves our capacity for problem-solving.

Every time my radar sends me warnings and I feel triggered, I assess if those emotions, beliefs, or expectations belong to me or are projected at me. 9 out of 10 times it's a projection.

When you are overwhelmed by someone else's drama, raise your hand (literally or figuratively) and say, "STOP. This does not belong to me."

(Thank you, Hélène, for this lovely saying that activates healthy boundaries!)

13. Shine On—Finding My Treasure

Align your Motivation with Passion

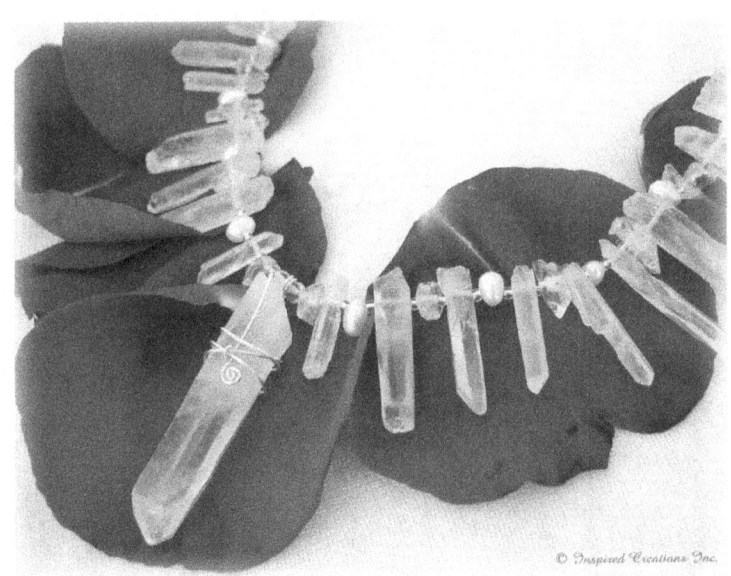

> *"We don't outgrow people, relationships, and situations, we outgrow versions of ourselves which are no longer in alignment with them"* –Unknown

I sat outside on the steps of the manufacturing plant where I worked, with my inhaler in one hand and grabbing my chest with the other. I was having a full-blown asthma attack and trying to relax my airways. Wheezing, I looked up at the trees and tried to clear my throat. I never wanted to step back into that place.

The feeling when you go into an asthma attack or anaphylactic shock is terrifying. Your throat closes off, you can't breathe so you slowly suffocate. In the worst case scenario, you must use a lifesaving EpiPen for its adrenaline to dilate your blood vessels and open your airways. I've used mine a few times. It's frightening. Humans can only survive three minutes without air.

That morning, the asthma attack was a reaction to whichever herbal supplement the plant was processing. You could smell it in the offices from the production side. It was extremely unpleasant and my reaction could have been worse.

At the time, I was fighting an unknown auto-immune disease* and started reacting to many environmental factors. I had resorted to using my inhaler the last time I visited the office, and today been forced to wear a mask to work. I still ended up gasping on the doorstep after three puffs of Albuterol.

I looked up to an especially gorgeous sky and snickered.

I was literally allergic to my work.

If that message wasn't strong enough, I was clueless!

I hated being there and had zero interest in what was initially a creative graphic design job but turned into a stressful deadline-driven management position of juggling packaging suppliers, production schedules, and clients' artwork. I had been very sick the last few years and looking for a job because my lack of passion didn't fit up high on my priority list. Plus, four days out of the week I was allowed to work from the boat. Back then, you were part of a special league if you landed such a job.

I also lacked the courage to quit, afraid of being out of work. I felt stuck and defeated. My sole motivation was money. We still had a huge boat loan to pay, and I had placed our financial security over my welfare and was paying for it now.

None of this mattered anymore because my body said, "enough" and forced me out. It wasn't a joke; I was allergic to this place.

Instead of feeling deflated, my spirit took a deep breath while my lungs waited to catch up. No matter my fears, I had to make a change.

I remember looking at the pretty puffy clouds and the city around me fell quiet, the loading docks were empty and everyone inside worked oblivious to my struggle. I listened to my body and in a clear loud voice I heard:

"WHAT THE HELL ARE YOU DOING HERE?"

I got up, grabbed my car keys, and drove away.

When you don't know what to do—the only thing to figure out is step one. My step one was leaving a toxic environment.

My boss tried to coax me to come back, but I heard my body's message loud and clear. I was never going to put my health in jeopardy again. So, I asked myself, "Now, what?"

I was done multitasking between label quotes, emails, and chasing clients. How ridiculously devoid of joy these tasks were for me. Maybe my depression wasn't because I was chronically ill, couldn't channel my creativity, and disliked my job. Maybe I was sick because my spirit was deflated, and couldn't find anything to be passionate about.

I needed to have fun again! How could I earn a living while doing something fun and work from the boat?

I needed to find what brought me joy.

For the first time in my work life, I didn't have a fallback plan and I wanted to leave the commercial graphics design behind. Burned out on deadlines and stress, I needed a change.

I had been dipping my toes in the holistic and self-development world for the last few years as I attempted to heal myself and learned all kinds of cool things. It amazed me that so many factors could affect my well-being, and no one had ever mentioned those to me before I got sick.

For me, I found that energy work, intuition, creativity, chakras, breath work, stress relief, mindfulness, yoga, and meditation were my joy—my soul was lit up when I sat in that sphere! They brought me comfort in a very cloudy period of my life.

I didn't want to feel this joy only on certain occasions, I wanted to feel it all the time. These practices opened an inner door and the wonder

I felt walking that path was electrifying. Now, I wanted more out of life, and everything, including work, to reflect wellness, and happiness.

Since my boss gave me an ultimatum to either work on the premises (even rescinding the option of continuing to work from home) or consider myself fired. I obviously could not continue for medical reasons, thus, I qualified for unemployment. This gave me a lifeline while I changed my life.

I felt a huge weight lift from my shoulders and energized for the first time in a very long time. I was just starting to listen to my intuition, and it was hard to decipher if the inner voice had my best interest at heart and if I was making the right decisions. I knew that I needed to do something creative to be happy and somehow tie it to wellness.

I had started making beach jewelry the year before. In the Keys, lovely sea beans (sometimes called hamburger beads) washed ashore that floated over from South America and Africa. They were different sizes and colors of reds, tans, and black. We collected them and my friend showed me how to drill them and make necklaces. I also wire-wrapped shark teeth and strung seashells. It was fun and everyone I knew loved wearing them. Soon after, my yogi friends introduced me to the healing benefits of gemstones, and I was hooked. My hobby blossomed into a passion for jewelry design. I graduated from fossils to gemstones and from shells to Swarovski crystals.

I've loved playing with stones ever since my mom first showed me my grandfather's rock collection as a kid. When I beaded and worked with crystals, time stopped. It was like a form of meditation that quieted my mind. I was lost in beautiful semi-precious rocks—a gift from the earth—and used their colors, brilliance, and properties to create 3D artworks.

Mmmmm…

A plan was forming…

Chapter 13 — Align your Motivation with Passion

I had furthered my Reiki training becoming a master, at first to heal myself and then to share its benefits with others. I loved the practice and knew that I could combine its effects with gemstones. I needed the energy of Reiki and crystals in my life as much as the people I would sell these beauties to. Designing wearable art truly inspired me and my creativity needed an outlet. It was a leap, even for me. But the idea lit me up.

"I am going to start a Reiki Infused Crystal Jewelry business," I told myself. Joining my current passions for healing, Reiki, and gemstones. I would finally be doing something I love. Oh, what a breath of fresh air.

I charted a new course and felt energized by my new goal. It was about time this pirate got a treasure chest full of gems onboard. I would align and shine!

*(see book 1)

LESSON: Align your motivation with passion
You can be aligned in many ways: with the philosophy of your boss, the goals of your workplace, the beliefs of your church, the politics of your government, the teachings of your coach or guru, etc. Above all else, it is essential is to be in alignment with yourself, your passion, and your deepest desires. This is the only way to stay motivated through thick and thin. Other people's goals or financial gain is not enough for deep-seated happiness.

When I thought about using my creative talents to design jewelry I was filled with an overwhelming sense of joy and purpose. I even felt lighter. If feelings were a guide, this was my new North, and everything pointed to this being my next step.

This, I was passionate about. This resonated with me. This inspired me after a long period of darkness. It didn't matter if this was a flight of fancy, a temporary gig, or a long-term plan. What mattered was that it got me unstuck from a place that wasn't good for me and motivated me to move toward a future that energized me.

Passion is associated with our second chakra, the sacral chakra, and motivation is associated with our third chakra, the solar plexus.

QUESTION: What moves and motivates me?

 ACTION: Create your sun mantra mandala

Draw a circle in the middle of a piece of paper and add straight long lines around it as if representing the sun and its rays.

In the middle of the sun, write *I align with...*

On the rays, write all the things that you truly align with in your life.

For example: I align with spirituality, slowing down, eating healthy, exercising, healing my body, spending more time in nature, supportive clients with easy deadlines, introspective mornings, journaling, activism, spirituality, inspiring books and TV programs, encouraging friends, freedom of choice, purposeful work, adventures, beach activities, gardening, puppies and animals, deep conversations with friends, maintain a healthy body weight, traveling retreats, etc.

These are the things that light you up, your sources of positive energy that radiate into your life. Make sure you get plenty of rays every day because it sustains your well-being. Write these in the positive tense, rather than the negative tense. For example, do

Chapter 13 — Align your Motivation with Passion

not write "less work," "not seeing someone," or "losing weight," etc. "Less," and "not" are negative words. Rather, use words like "more free time," "great friends," or "healthy weight." The brain does not differentiate between positive and negative words and registers every word you say or write. (This is important to apply to your speech as well.) Besides, the sun radiates positivity. Turn this into your Sun Mantra Mandala.

14 - Orgasmic Stars— Riding the Big One

Align your Shakti Energy

> *"The deepest source of love is found within. Shower the world with it."* —Carole

When we were young, we couldn't keep our hands off each other. Those first rushed encounters in a passionate love affair when you can't tear your clothes off fast enough, and you look at each other afterward, disheveled, and out of breath, then crack up at what just happened. That was us. It was so intense; it was insane. We were insatiable and adventurous in our encounters, impatient and daring in our locations.

After that first kiss, our crazy love took off like a supersonic jet to the moon. Two pieces of a puzzle—connected—life together suddenly made sense. We made sense. Sex was out of this world.

Early in our relationship, we spent hours exploring each other's bodies, seducing our souls with burning desire and sensual lovemaking. Our passion could only be tamed by the complete possession of each other's bodies and souls. Only then could our needs be satisfied.

Then, we'd spend the rest of the night pillow-talking until dawn sharing every detail and secret of our lives. Physical intimacy awakened our need to be seen, touched, held, and connected, and it opened our hearts to deep emotional intimacy.

After decades together—20 of them on a 41' monohull—we became so close that we ended each other's sentences and knew the other often better than we knew ourselves. Our intensity may have diminished over the years but the passion still lights up our lives.

Although we loved taking friends and family on sailing trips, most of the time we sailed alone. While the world was busy with lattes, commutes, meetings, and politics, we escaped to the sea where time chased after the sun, and we were free to live out fantasies, exploring sights rarely seen by anyone.

We found ourselves walking through spells where each would be lost in thoughts as if moving in a trance inspired by our deep immersion in this flowing aquatic world. Words were unnecessary. We acted as one, knowing how to capture the wind and master our elements. We knew each other's habits, watch schedules, moods, and chores. We floated in a timeless capsule.

One of my favorite things to do was to look up at the stars. I bought a Stars and Planets Guide [5] that gave me detailed charts of the sky for each hemisphere, time zone, or month of the year, so I could play junior astronomer and gaze at the stars knowing the movement and location of the constellations.

This was the first trip after we had a sturdy hardtop installed over the cockpit. Sailboats usually had flimsy canvas tops covering the cockpit to give the captain protection from the weather. Material, zippers, and straps had to be maintained and did not survive many harsh tropical seasons. After a few replacements (ripped from the burning sun or shredded by Hurricane Irene), we tired of the recurring expense and tapped our savings to splurge on a permanent solution. We were the proud owners of a badass enclosure for Windsong; it was a solid, custom-designed, aluminum and honeycomb fiberglass ceiling with premium clear Strataglass™ windows. It was an absolute beauty. It raised the top almost a foot giving us more headspace at the helm and

Chapter 14 — Align your Shakti Energy

walking in the cockpit and was supported by the same large piping as tuna towers on sportfishing boats. The great thing about it was that it held the weight of three adults and ladder steps were designed within the structure to climb on top so we could access the perfect suntanning salon and/or balcony to the stars. We could also tend to our sail from above.

We were anchored miles away from civilization next to a small, secluded island that was merely a dot on our chart. We were the only humans in sight. Overhead, the stunning Milky Way exposed by darkness shone brighter than imaginable and took up most of the sky above. Rarely do people get the chance to admire our galaxy in a clear, real-life, 3-D view, her canvas typically hidden by manmade lights. The arching celestial arm drew colors, and stars in the sky with magnificent depth.

It was profoundly awe-inspiring. So much that it didn't look real. I had never witnessed anything more revealing about how tiny our life was on this blue and green planet.

We grabbed blankets and pillows and climbed up. Eric swung the main boom and sail, and shackled them to the side rail. This gave us the whole elevated platform to stargaze. We laid down looking up at our 360°degree private planetarium. Imagine being on a silent stage surrounded by endless sky and ocean as far as the eyes can see. While it was silent, the quietness felt charged with life. Only the peaceful sound of water softly lapped the hull. The smooth expanse glistened like a brilliant mirror and reflected this canopy along with a big bright moon. Traveling waves barely large enough to distort this reflection gently swayed Windsong in a soothing motion. They temporarily captured us, rolling all around our boat, then broke away and released their grip to continue their journey rolling across the sea.

I felt deeply connected. Mother Nature held us in her arms. We were a part of it. Nowhere else was it more evident or inclusive. The sea connected us to every distant shore on earth. The vastness of our surrounding space was inebriating. The ocean extended from horizon to horizon all around us, an unending canvas transcending space with the rich dark sky contrasting with illuminating stars. You could not tell where the sky ended and where the water began except for the slight undulation in its reflection. I almost felt like we were out in space, floating high on this platform with several hundred billion stars surrounding me. It was mesmerizing.

Our only witnesses were the sea creatures, dolphins, turtles, fish, and whales I knew inhabited these waters. I sensed a fullness in my heart and completely melted in gratitude for bearing witness to this. I scanned the sky for specific stars and constellations like the Northern Cross, and the Big Dipper, knowing great navigators from long ago relied on the same ones I traced with my finger in the night sky.

It was warm and we cozied up with cushions on our blanket, stargazing like teenagers. I could taste the salty air on my lips and kissed Eric. I experienced the clearest and deepest connection with him. Being there together and witnessing this sight transcended time. Although we were alone right there and then, I had the sudden realization that we were undoubtedly connected with everything, everywhere, and part of this gigantic ever-moving live Universe.

The beauty and grandeur of life hit me. I felt love encircle us and expand a million miles large to include everyone and everything in nature. The magic was palpable. The stardust ran through my veins and pulsated with life.

I quivered and turned to my husband with passion and fury. I needed to connect and experience this cosmic moment on an intimate and orgasmic level. To be a part of and move with this energy. I felt an immense sense of being-ness. Me being me, with him inside of me—we were whole—completely part of this grand Universe, tiny specks we may be, but connected and part of it all, nonetheless. I could breathe this life forever.

His experienced touch made me wild. All my senses were in hyperdrive. Like antennas tapping into this cosmic vibe. The sensations were impossible to contain, and a surge of energy exploded inside of me. I felt wave after wave of ecstasy. Torn wide open and without holding back, I gave myself completely. For the first time in my life, I felt my cries and essence expand and in a nanosecond, my boundaries shattered, a gateway opened, and I broke out of my body. Time and space didn't exist, only being-ness. I became a wave of energy connected across the ethers reaching the farthest corners of the Universe. The vastness was me; I became limitless. One with the stellar stars.

Just. Fucking. Wow.

In absolute nakedness, my spirit soared. Indescribable bliss. I was having an orgasmic out-of-body experience. I embraced it all. Loved it all. Saw it all. Embodied it all.

We must have sent shockwaves reverberating across the water and I wondered if the sea creatures felt the echoes.

To love under a blanket of stars, hearts wide open, so raw, so pure, so human, so natural, and so connected with nature, all with the universe staring down at us. I was part of the Light, and for a moment, traveled back to it. Time stopped.

Covered in starlight, and caressed by the night, I embraced my lover, grateful for his help in harnessing this powerful Kundalini* wave.

---

*Kundalini energy which resides at the base of the spine is considered a type of shakti energy. It can be raised to travel up the spine, through our chakras, up to our crown and out to connect with Source.

Married sex is rarely this intense—this was epic cosmic love.

In heightened awareness, I was flooded with a deep reverence for destiny, the planet, and all living beings. Life could not get any better than this.

LESSONS: Align your shakti energy

Shakti energy is the feminine creative force in all the Universe. It permeates every cell, and every atom, animating life, connecting us, moving through us, emanating from objects, trees, all living beings, and Mother Earth. It is the water cascading down the rivers and the life force flowing in us, our essence, our energy, our spark—and Source's ("God's") conscious spirit playing in this three-dimensional world. It is the vibration of life, carried in our breath, giving us life. It is our chi and our life force in action.

Our sacral or sexual chakra located below our navel and over our sexual organs is the seat of our creative force and governs relationships and emotions. Creation doesn't only come in the form of making babies, you need creative energy for goals, innovations, art, and every creation you imagine.

It does not matter whether or not you have a womb. Men have this same chakra to propel their creations too. And, even if you've had a hysterectomy like me, this is still your energetic center. It is our center of creation and is located in the same area for men and women.

When our lower and higher chakras are fully opened and the energy can flow without blockages from the base of the spine to the top of the head, one can feel immense surges of energy, creativity, inspiration, intuition, wisdom, and be in complete union with Spirit and Source.

When I got sick, I was in physical pain from multiple surgeries and disconnected from my lower chakra. This stopped the flow of my creative power. I also had stagnation in other chakras. I fell into a rut, felt stuck, and got depressed.

Aligning and nurturing this critical chakra helped me create a more balanced life.

Notice how relaxed and inspired you feel after an orgasm. It is one of the greatest gifts we have been given. Do not discard the power of connection and healing that lovemaking can provide. Inhabit your body with full awareness in the moment. When orgasming, there is no past or future, no worries or judgment, no stress or anxiety, only sensations and presence. Climax erases all boundaries of time, space, and thoughts.

If you are sensitive to energy, you can feel the orgasmic waves roll through your body clearing away blockages and leaving in its wake an immense sense of release and completion. As you move through multiple orgasms, each one brings you deeper into your energy line.

There are many ways to balance your sacral chakra but for the sake of this story, I am exploring the sexual aspect of the second chakra.

I cannot speak for men, but for heightened pleasure, a woman must be in alignment to fully open and embrace her sexual experience. Your partner may not always be in alignment with what you need, so communication is key.

Intimate relationships grow, change with time and age, fluctuate with moods, cycles, and our sexuality matures as our needs change. Honoring and aligning our sexuality with where we are at in the present moment is essential for a healthy sacral chakra.

Align with what feels good to you. Affirm what you desire. Allow only what makes you feel comfortable while remaining curious and willing to participate. There is no shame in the ways you want to be loved, as long as no one gets hurt, and you are consenting adults. Sex is not bad, dirty, or wrong. It is the most natural thing there is, and you have the right to express your sexuality any way you want. Your desires are nothing to be embarrassed about and your sexuality should be celebrated.

Be creative in your lovemaking, what felt good years ago may not be so today. Remain respectful of your body and embrace your cycles. Being sick made me appreciate my body like never before. There was a time I did not know If I would be able to ever feel this way again. I have a whole new appreciation for the human body's ability to heal. Care for your body wholeheartedly.

Be with someone who fully embraces and loves every inch of you, from your quirky flaws to everything you feel self-conscious about.

When two people are aligned with each other, and with their sexual energy and desires, sex can be soul-satisfying, and quench a thirst for connection like nothing else. There is no greater connection between two human beings than when we are fully present with each other in the act of lovemaking. To experience absolute orgasmic energy, one must be willing to let go of all barriers between the two souls and connect as one, at least for a brief moment in time.

Sex is the most physical joy you can express and receive in this incarnate body. What can be bad about something we call ecstatic and orgasmic? And why wouldn't you want to explore or express it? It is the only way our species survives so of course it is written in our DNA and ingrained in our deepest unconscious desires.

Is there anything better in this world than having an orgasm with someone you love?

Seriously. Orgasms are free, you always carry everything you need with you everywhere you go, you can do it by yourself or share with others, for a moment it makes you forget all your worries, it makes you feel extraordinary, releases stress, gives you a boost of energy, instantly changes your vibe, can uplift even the worse day, gives you a beautiful glow, it's great cardio, and afterward your happiness is contagious. Did I mention that it's free?

And remember, you don't need a partner. Although it's fun to share in the joy with a partner, orgasms through masturbation help dissipate energy blockages—proven to ease migraines and more. It's a reset button, flooding your body with happy hormones and dispersing energy helping you feel more equalized, relaxed, and balanced. Whether with a partner or on your own, climax is nature's gift of ecstasy. And if anyone ever tells you to go fuck yourself, you can honestly answer, *"With pleasure."*

A note on sexual healing... Many women (and men) have experienced some type of trauma or harassment related to their sexuality. I sympathize. I have too. Please do not ignore or discard your sex life because of such experiences. A sex therapist can help you reconnect with your body so that you can reach climax without the negative imprint this may have left behind. There is hope as you rebuild the trust between you and your orgasms. Contact your licensed healthcare practitioner if you experience pain or discomfort during intercourse, and explore alternate forms of lovemaking.

QUESTION: This is what I want from my lover:
Ask your spouse: How do you want me to love you?

 ACTION: Sexy date with yourself
Close the curtains and explore what your body likes. Allow yourself to receive pleasure. You can only be satisfied by your lover if you know what you enjoy. You can only know if you try it. There is nothing dirty about sex. Worth repeating; there is NOTHING dirty about sex or masturbation.

Sexy date as a couple
If you are not physical with your partner at least once a week, make a date, it could be as simple as choosing a song you enjoy to slow dance, or giving each other massages, and entering each other's aura.

15. Detours—Close Call with a Sea Monster

Align Feelings and Emotions

"An optimal course is rarely linear." —Carole

We always resisted being tethered to land and waited until the last minute to sail back to the mainland, squeezing every week, day, and second out of our precious time in the islands, and risked putting ourselves in a precarious position on our journey home. That was the plight of the sailor who had a land job to support his dream. It was our choice to race against less than optional conditions so when we reluctantly sailed back toward the US and the ocean was chaotic, we had no choice but to batten down the hatches and hold on for a rough passage.

I previously mentioned that when sailing from the Bahamas to Florida, we had to cross the offshore prevailing current moving south to north, called the Gulf Stream. It was like crossing a 30 miles wide flowing river—inside the ocean—with a current of approximately 2.5 knots (2.9 mph). When we had a southernly wind, the seas were usually calmer because it blew in the same direction as the current. The more the wind veered to the north, the more it clashed against the current and waves, creating choppy and dangerous seas.

Our course ran 299° degrees from Bimini to Fort Lauderdale. We had to compensate for the fast current by steering Windsong an extra 25° degrees south to make up for the drift to point toward home. That meant that once we hit the Gulf Stream, the current slowed us down, and we barely made 2 to 3 knots. We had crashing waves on deck, and a 15-knots wind almost on the nose. Because of the conditions of the seas, this was the best and quickest option for us to our destination unless we tacked northwest where we'd end up somewhere in Central Florida and lose hours motoring back south once we got into coastal waters. And even then, we'd still have the wind on our bow, just less chop. This was the least uncomfortable course to sail.

A sailboat can only be steered while making way. The faster we sailed, the better we could steer the boat. The slower we went, the less maneuverable or accurate we were in guiding Windsong, and the more dangerous it became, especially in confused seas. Wind, current, and waves, either helped us surf faster or added resistance and slowed us down.

We were experienced sailors by this time and had boated through similar conditions, so we were prepared for the trip ahead, settled in our respective seats and held on as comfortably as we could. As long as we kept this heading, we made slow progress but we'd be home before dark.

That's when a 220,000-ton dark metal monster appeared on the horizon barreling down the sea.

We were crossing the international shipping lanes. The invisible highways only seen on charts that freighters and large commercial vessels use to travel from port to port, and across the world. The sea lanes follow trade winds and prevailing currents and are the busiest part of the sea.

For a small vessel like ours, (41 feet is considered small) it was best to avoid navigating anywhere close to them to avoid collision because large ships are much less maneuverable than a little boat. Changing course on a 220,000-ton container ship that is sailing at 20 knots, took miles to accomplish, so we had best get out of their way.

Chapter 15 — Align Feelings and Emotions

I was lucky to experience the life-size simulator at the STAR center in Dania Beach—a leading maritime training center in the USA for deck and engineer officers—where we clearly saw how these vessels are extremely slow to react and maneuver. Even after having been forewarned in the simulator, we ended up crushing a private vessel and crashing into port.

Eric and I started to plot both ships' courses and tried to figure out who was going to cross in front of the other at the speed we were sailing. At this point, we were barely making way and being slammed left and right, up, and down, in 8 to 10-foot seas. In this weather, we had to steer our vessel in the safest possible direction so as not to risk damaging the boat, getting swamped, or hurting ourselves. This was it. The last thing we wanted to do was change Windsong's course and take on the rough seas while we broke everything inside and held on for dear life.

Sailboats under sail generally have right of way over motorboats because of their restricted maneuverability but that doesn't include ships and freighters. The maritime rules say that whenever two vessels arrive at the same point at the same time, whichever boat has the other boat on its starboard side must give way. So, even though we were sailing in dangerous seas, we were the stand-down boat.

The problem was that we had no idea of their speed and whether they planned on crossing in front of us, or behind us, or when the crossing would happen. We were like a small yellow duck in a washing machine. We barely had enough power to stay our course.

The 220,000-metal monster crept closer. Tension was rising on board as we clearly saw the freighter rise from the horizon and start to darken the sky. A huge container ship fully loaded at maximum speed could run over a sailboat like ours, and not even feel a thing. In fact, I heard a story of a freighter coming to port with remnants of a sailboat stuck on the bulbous bow of container ships when they arrived in port. The captain never knew they had hit a vessel.

We tried to raise the captain on the VHF radio to ask if their instruments told them if we were on a collision course.

"Security, Security, Security. This is the sailing vessel Windsong calling the southbound freighter located at latitudes and longitudes XX. Please come in."

We couldn't see anyone on board through our binoculars and the airwaves were dead.

"Security, Security, Security. This is the sailing vessel Windsong calling southbound freighter at latitudes and longitudes XX. Come in, please. Can you confirm your speed and if you will cross in front or behind our vessel? Please state your intentions and speed, over."

We radioed for half an hour; no one answered.

Commercial ships must maintain a watch on channel 16 while underway, and answer calls when being hailed at sea. They were also supposed to always have a person on watch posted while at sea to avoid collision and/or render aid if necessary. But freighters rarely adhere to these laws, and never or rarely answer the calls of a private vessel.

This monstrous ghost ship was forging dead ahead, with its thousands of pounds of cold dark metal, and we were on a path to annihilation.

We weren't about to play chicken with them, but we needed to stay on our course as long as possible and veer off last minute because once we changed course, we would be thrown into mayhem and struggle to maintain safety on our boat.

We slowed Windsong down as much as we could without losing steering and planned on letting them pass in front of us, without getting swamped. The wind was howling, and we had two out of three sails opened. The time and hazard of changing directions for longer than necessary was not worth the risks of tacking and putting the boat (and

Chapter 15 — Align Feelings and Emotions

crew) under more stress. If we pointed to the wind to tack, we would lose complete motion and be at the mercy of the sea—and the oncoming ship.

Suddenly the ride was extremely uncomfortable. The boat was slamming hard against the waves and rolling side to side. The wind flopped in our sails but still filled them enough to make small progress. We could hear the crashing sound of items down below. Dishes and provisions slid in the cupboards and personal items were thrown on the floor. My poor dog Dingo who hated rough seas was giving us the evil eye hiding in the corner.

A chill breezed through the air as the creaking metallic freighter sailed barely 200 feet in front of us. It was a monster of a wall clouding up the whole horizon. By now, we had changed directions at the last minute and aimed Windsong directly at the ship and into the path of the crashing wake it created. My dog threw up. Then he pooped on the cockpit carpet. Poor thing had already taken homeopathics for seasickness earlier, but this carnival ride was too much for his sensitive stomach. The sight and smell made our salty legs turn a bit queasy. It was a messy, stinky, scary situation.

Imagine an approximately 12-story high building as wide as a small neighborhood block sails in front of you at about 20 to 25nm (23-28.5mph/37-46 km) creating a huge wake of churning water with its displacement.

The fully loaded container ship crashed into the waters as it made its way ahead of us. Its enormity temporarily cast a shadow on Windsong's crew and even snuffed the wind from our sails. We could see every scratch on the hull and cranked our necks to see any signs of life on the deck high above. None. It was deserted. I held on for dear life as I tried to clean up Dingo's mess with one hand and squeezed my legs against the cockpit hull for balance. The carpet was "lost" at sea.

Ouf, what a ride. Our captain blasted curses at the sea monster and its invisible crew as we took on the extra 10 foot waves the container ship threw at us. These ships displace an enormous amount of water that sends huge waves, which made an already bad sea worse.

The ghost ship forged ahead as if nothing happened. Oblivious to the fact that it gave these two sailors one of the most rock'n rolling hours in their sailing lives. We would live to boogie and sail another day.

It took us another 30 minutes to re-adjust our direction so that we settled in a choppy but endurable position and left the trail of the drooling wake behind. My dog settled down for a well-deserved nap nestled between two cushions, while a ration of rum settled the captain's nerves.

Constant vigilance, awareness, and knowing your true course are essential for a successful journey at sea, as is true in life

LESSON: Align feelings and emotions

Sometimes determining my true course in life is even more difficult than on a raging sea. It helps me to understand the difference between my feelings and my emotions which gives me a new perspective on challenges. This emotional intelligence helps me put emotional distance between myself and the perceived "obstacle."

We say the word "feel" for both feelings and emotions, but they are two separate things.

EMOTIONS are sensory-based and start with physical sensations, like butterflies in your stomach, expansion or tightness in the chest, the welling of tears in the eyes, or the raising of hair on the arms. What the body senses triggers chemical reactions and sends signals to the brain. (E= "energy in"–MOTION)

FEELINGS are the stories that the mind creates when interpreting those emotions, like "I'm scared we're going to hit a rock," "I'm sad about not landing the job," or "I'm excited to dinghy to shore."

You are neither your feelings nor emotions—no matter how intense or overwhelming they may feel. You are a human being who is simply <u>experiencing</u> them. Both will pass. The ocean does not define herself by the currents that run through her. Do not define yourself by feelings running through you. Breathe and connect with the sensations in your body, choose to be fully present with the senses, instead of focusing on the stories.

The mind-driven feelings are the ones that usually get us in trouble and are what most people align with. My inner chatter and fears hijack my reasoning and steer me in the wrong direction. When I lead by my senses and respond to my body's intelligence, I make better, healthier decisions. If my body feels tight and contracted it's a "no" and if it feels open and light, it's a "yes."

You can change the narrative inside your head. Use awareness to align yourself with your emotions (senses) it will heighten your intuition. Your body has your best interest at heart–literally!

---

*For more on body talk see page 213 in Book 1 to decipher your body's language.

QUESTION: If I am being truthful, I really feel...

 ACTION: YES / NO game

Learn to recognize the subtle signs for how your body answers "yes" or "no" to everything in life. One way to practice this is by holding objects or reading statements.

Put a few miscellaneous objects within reach. Close your eyes and take a few deep breaths. Notice your body's sensations. Take one object into your hands and state out loud what the object is. For example: "This is my cup." Then say, "Yes, yes, yes," out loud. Feel how the truth resonates in your body. Possibly a light feeling of openness and relaxation. Sit with sensations for a minute and familiarize yourself with your "yes" feeling.

Now, holding the same object, make a false statement about it. For example: while holding a cup say, "This is a cake," followed by, "No, no, no," out loud. Feel how being inauthentic resonates in your body. Possibly a feeling of contraction, tightness of belly, or heaviness on your shoulders. Sit with sensations for a minute and familiarize yourself with your "no" feeling.

Practice saying true and false statements (holding objects helps in the beginning) and become an expert at reading your "yes" and your "no."

16. Provisioning Tale—A Soda Trail

Align with Flexibility

Our two explorers Eric and Jean-Pierre.

*"Eeny, meeny, miny, moe, in what directions should I go?
To port side the sunset glows, starboard side the moon
follows. Captain stubbed his big right toe, that's a sign and
now I know." —Carole*

Our party cruise of four woke up somewhere in the Abacos to an emerging emergency: we were almost out of Coca-Cola to go along the daily rum rations for happy hour. Please note, in those days, happy hour *might* have started on European time and ended on Hawaiian time.

Despite our best efforts filling all nooks and crannies on the boat with everything we thought we would need to travel with our guests. Our friends Jean-Pierre and Gina joked when they climbed aboard that there wasn't space left for clothes. Semi-jokingly, we replied, "Good thing you only need their bathing suits from this point on." But having miscalculated our libation/chaser ratio, now that was no joke at all.

Cause for concern; we had a serious Pan-Pan emergency. (Pronounced "pahn-pahn" from the French word "panne" meaning "broke down or stalled," it is used when calling for special attention on the VHF radio channel when a situation is non-life-threatening, but you can't continue forward without assistance.) We could not continue forward without Coca-Cola.

So, the men told the women, "Don't worry, you enjoy the sun and we—manly man—will jump in the dinghy and go hunt on the nearest island."

They left and dinghied around for a while trying to find signs of civilization and found a small dock with a single occupant, an old black Bahamian man with white hair sitting and fishing, hoping for a nice catch for lunch.

The guys smiled and pulled over, "Hello mister, we're looking for a convenience store where we can buy some Cokes. Any around here?" The old chap looked at them with a slightly surprised look and said, "Yeahhh, ther a store up tha way in th' back." Waving them further along.

Unsure of how far he meant, Eric tells JP, "I'll go this direction by dinghy, and you take the dog and the trash and go by foot by the road."

(A trip to shore is never done without the opportunity to 1) walk the dog, and 2) take the garbage off Windsong.)

JP found himself alone, on foot, on some island he didn't even know the name of, with our dog, Dingo in tow, still wearing his tiny yellow life vest with a large black carrying hook on top. JP held a retractable leash in one hand, and carried a large trash bag on his opposite shoulder. It was the end of July in the Bahamas so it wasn't hot—it was scorching hot. Once off the dinghy, the air was stagnant and stifling, so our friend walked shirtless, sweaty, holding a large black garbage bag that was a bit stinky, and despite being the middle of the day, mosquitos were everywhere. Wearing tattoos, a goatee, large gold earrings in both ears, Teva's on his feet, Hawaiian board shorts, and sunburn, JP looked displaced and displeased in his biker-turned-sailor touristy getup. This pre-sparrow pirate pulled down his straw hat and hit the road looking for bounty.

Chapter 16 — Align with Flexibility

Fontaine made his way around the point to try to find the store via water and lost sight of his buddy after a few minutes.

JP went down the dirt road with a determined walk when a highly suspicious-looking black car with dark tinted windows drove by. He heard the loud rap music blasting out as it slowed down at crawling speed right next to him like they were staking him out, but he could not see inside. The car passed by and kept going leaving a trail of dust in its wake. He breathed a sigh of relief. Then he saw the red brake lights, and the car stopped. It reversed and slowly backed his way.

"Damn," he thought to himself. "I have too much s&%t to handle right now, not here, not now. I'm on vacation for God's sake." As he waved some mosquitoes away. The black sedan lowered the windows and a cloud of smoke puffed out of the car. JP recognized the ganga smell and saw his stalkers: four Bahamians dressed Miami Vice style, wearing heavy gold chains, and flashy sunglasses—island mafia style—who smiled at him and called out,

"Hey man, ya want some ganga?" "No thanks." JP answered, relieved that it was a sales call, instead of a shakedown. "All right, man." They left. Sigh.

He saw the red brake lights again. Here they came again, slowly backing up. "Now what?" JP thought.

The driver asked, "Yo! What's that ya caarrying on ya shoulder, man?"

"It's my garbage, I came by boat." JP replied.

"Where ya going with ya garbage?" They chuckled.

"Well, I'm looking for a place to throw it out." JP informed.

207

The driver repeated and snickered. "He looking for a place to throw his trash. Man, Ha! Ha! Ha!" They echoed and rolled with laughter. "Throw 'it right there in the ditch like we do!" pointing to the side of the road with bewildered faces.

He could still hear them laugh as they sped away. Some islands—unfortunately to this day—are not great at sanitation.

Well, he didn't get mugged and gave the islanders great comedy relief. Win-Win.

He made it to the convenience store glad to see his wingman waving at him. Eric had found a pier completely made out of large conch shells and docked beside it.

The small convenience store was a respite from the sun's heat and their trek, and they entered eager to supply their mission. When their eyes adjusted to the dimness, they saw a young girl of maybe ten or twelve years old manning the store from behind the counter. They walked up to her and asked in typical tourist lingo, "We'd like four twelve packs of coke, please."

The little girl looked at them and silently pointed to the 10 cans in the store's window.

"No, we don't want 4 cans, we want *4 boxes,* please."

"Ya don't understand, mister," she said, "this is all we have in the store." Pointing to the meager bounty. The guys looked at each other in surprise and then scanned the store to see half-empty shelves everywhere. They felt bad for the folks and didn't want to take their whole stash of soda—so they took eight and left two cans behind. They grabbed a bag of ice, a luxury onboard Windsong, and paid their tab.

Off they went to the dock and left the miserably muggy and buggy island. They didn't get mugged; they got bugged!

Chapter 16 — Align with Flexibility

They climbed aboard and Dingo's coat was full of mosquitos. Poor thing. Once they spotted you, they were on you to suck you dry. You couldn't hide from them, they followed like vampires on prey. There was no way the guys could dinghy to the boat this way or else we'd have stowaways the rest of the trip. They would have to ditch the itch!

As soon as they were away from the dock, Eric stabbed the little motor at full speed to try to lose their wings. Our motley crew deserved a cold one for their efforts that day. But their plight wasn't over. The voracious little beasts were not 125cc normal skeeters, they were supercharged V turbo engines buzzing for their goal, and they were out for blood. Our manley-mens' blood.

They had to zig-zag far away from Windsong to shake off their tail— we thought they were being playful and waved at them in the distance— while they were brushing off Dingo's fur, their hair, and clothes to get rid of unwanted stowaways. JP joked that if any remained on board, they could fill our sails with a flap of their wings.

By the time our duo finally landed onboard, they were overheated from their excursion and looking forward to having a cold one. They opened the cooler, and took out eight cans of Coke and a large bag of dripping water! Cocktail hour would remain at tepid room temperature for yet another day.

The only one who got to chill that day was our furry crewmember, Dingo, who after having a nice walk sniffing to his heart's content, enjoyed a free grooming session with a cooling ride home—his favorite thing—with ears and tongue flapping in the wind *("Faster! Faster!")*, and got home to a boat well-stocked with his favorite treats *("Thank you, mama!")*, grateful for almost every new adventure. *("This was much better than a car ride, can we do it again, pleeeeazzze?!")*

LESSON: Align with flexibility

The Rolling Stones said it best: *"You can't always get what you want…but if you try sometimes, you'll find…you get what you need."* Sailing taught me to be flexible and adapt to change. The scarcity and limited on-the-water resources helped us develop our imagination, and rather than expecting life to always give us what we want, we learned to use what life brings us, welcome the alternatives, and make an adventure out of it.

Here are a few alternatives boaters and homemakers may enjoy:

1. Don't have eggs for a recipe? Here are three alternatives I always carried onboard, each is equivalent to one egg:
   - 3 tablespoons of the liquid from a can of chickpeas (called aquafaba)
   - Mix 1 tablespoon of ground flax seeds with 3 tablespoons of warm water. Let sit for 10 minutes
   - My favorite and a superfood, mix 1 tablespoon of chia seeds with 2.5 tablespoons water. Let sit for 15 minutes

2. Can't find lettuce? Cabbage keeps for weeks without refrigeration. Store uncovered in a well-ventilated space or wrapped in newspaper.

3. Don't have citrus or fresh herbs? Carry herbal and lemon extracts onboard, as well as Bragg's apple cider vinegar, or essence of vanilla, which makes a delicious soda-like mocktail when added to carbonated water.

4. Dehydrated foods are handy when meat and protein sources are unavailable. For example, organic textured soy protein is a delicious alternative in spaghetti sauce, and also makes great pizza sauce.

5. My husband is a mechanic and he wants to share the substitute he swears by. If you don't have disinfectant and you're in a jam, use PG1 brake cleaner or generic brands. It could save your hand from a phantom shark attack! (Yes, he's done that for years!)

QUESTION: Where and how can I be more flexible in life?

 ACTION: Flex your menu

For the next three weeks, I challenge you to eat something different for each dinner. That's right! Do not eat the same meal choice twice. Start by writing down ideas for 21 meals. This will help you realize how rigid—or open—you are in your eating habits. Notice how it feels to flex your I-can-try-new-things muscle. Learning to be flexible in one aspect of our lives can expand to other areas and help us become more adventurous and adaptive to whatever is on our plate.

17. Furbaby—My Salty Tail

Align your Tail with Wisdom

"Warf, rrrruff ruff grrr warwhar, wouf wouf, slurp, every time." —Dingo The Dog
(Translation: No matter how rocky the boat is, run for the treats, every chance you get.)

I was just a three-month-old puppy when my dad brought me home. He tucked me into his leather jacket and hopped on a loud machine he called Harley. He had a deep voice and laughed affectionately as I snuggled on his chest. I loved the smell of him and how my ears felt as the flip-flopped in the wind. I had never gone this fast before and could sense we were embarking on a great big adventure. I liked my new home, especially the pretty lady who scooped me up and kissed me all over, all the time. She had a lot of pretty friends who liked to hang around the pool in bikinis. I was the center of attention. They would take turns petting me and rubbing my belly, giving me treats, and throwing the ball for me. I lounged around in the shade under palm trees and had a high-rise dog-house large enough to play with the kids when they visited. I was the king of the house. These were the good old days.

Then, the daddy bought himself a strange doghouse. It was big, white, and had lots of leashes tied everywhere but no dogs. He kept it on wheels in the driveway and called it a sailboat. He worked on that thing for months, making a lot of noise and dust.

Then one day, the boss, my bikini mommy, a friend, and me went for a ride in the family moving machine. The doghouse was following us, and we all ended up at the beach. The boss rolled the doghouse in the water. I had a feeling I wasn't going to like it. Into the doghouse went the cooler, the music machine, and bags of tasty-smelling snacks. Hmmmm, it might not be so bad after all. So, I let the boss lift me and put me on the floating thing.

A funny feeling came over me as I tried to move—my paws slid—one went right, the other went left. What's this all about? Man, there better be some bacon treats in that bag. After maybe ten minutes I was doing better, woozy but better. Then the boss untied the leash of the floating doghouse and that's when I knew the day was going to hell. Tell me, what was the point of sitting in the middle of water? No trees to pee on? Being rocked every which way—my stomach couldn't even handle meatballs! Two big white sheets went up and for a while, the leashes were flapping all over the place as if phantom dogs were running insane. Scary thing! I wondered if we had demon dogs onboard. My bikini mommy took me on her lap and hugged me to comfort me. I noticed the clouds around and smelled rain in the air but didn't think of mentioning it to the boss; I was enjoying a nice petting.

It was getting rough, and I wasn't feeling better. I asked bikini mommy to help me below where I noticed they had decorated our kennel with fluffy cushions. I was looking forward to a nap.

Then suddenly everything jerked one way really hard. "Rotten steak and rubber bones! The doghouse was falling over!" Thrown to the floor I went, the bloody music machine fell on top of me and soon a human butt coming my way awfully fast, "NOOOOOOO! Ouch! That hurt." My very unhappy bikini mommy landed on top of me. I could hear the boss and his human called Wizard screaming in their big voices and heard them running around trying to grab the leashes that were flapping everywhere. Maybe the phantom dogs ran away. I wouldn't blame them. I wanted to run away, too. If we had a wizard onboard, couldn't he just make a spell to get out of this hell? The wind was howling now, and

Chapter 17 — Align your Tail with Wisdom

water was coming down from the skies. I could think of better places to be, like the pound! Next thing I knew, up came my breakfast—all over the floor. Maybe they wouldn't notice, I thought. After spinning around for a few circles, the boss announced that the doghouse was under control. We were on our way back to the dirt I so cherished.

Finally, some sense. This was a strange pack I belonged to. I would have to teach them a few things about using their puppy radar to get out of trouble.

The ride back to the land of the dogs was very wet and choppy. My paws didn't work on the white surface so I just stayed there standing on the cushion; swaying each way, my stomach in my throat, wishing I could wake up in the middle of Pet Supermarket. I looked like a rookie pup that chewed up his boss's sofa. Pitiful. We finally got back where we started, and the boss leashed the doghouse to the dead trees on the dock.

The wooziness left me and my tail went back up. I jumped on land and peed on every tree I could find, announcing that the king was back, and that, "THIS PUPPY SAVED THE DAY!"

No one needs to know the truth now, do they?

I really hate sailing.

Is that bacon I smell?"

Your favorite salty companion,

Dingo the Dog
AKA 1st Security Chief aboard Wannabe
(Presently sailing over the rainbow bridge.)

(Reporting on our first ocean sail aboard the family's first sailboat, a 25' MacGregor named Wannabe. Daddy Eric almost decided to end our sailing adventures that day—see book 1 for human version—thankfully, we went on to live many years in this great doghouse where I enjoyed a long life trampling many beaches. I retired at the best waterfront resort, and quietly crossed the rainbow bridge after many adventures.)

LESSON: Align your tail with wisdom

Some wisdom from our first furry boy...

- Never eat before Mommy and Daddy untie the doghouse
- Never lay below any large unsecured object
- When you smell rain, secure yourself
- A soft cushion makes almost anything bearable
- Never say no to a dinghy ride
- On landfalls, pee every chance you get
- Don't eat everything you smell
- Chewing on flip-flops is frowned upon
- When the flying sheets stop flopping, it's time for napping
- It's okay if land dogs don't believe your stories, keep your nose in the wind, catch the next wave, and make friends with water creatures!

QUESTION: What are my favorite treats? (Name all ways you treat yourself)

ACTION: Hugs make everything better

Dingo would tell you there's no shame in asking for hugs and cuddles when you need them.

According to Science, hugging for 20 seconds is enough to release happy hormones. [6] Physical contact, being touched, or held, not only soothes and calms, it lowers heart rate, blood pressure, and helps decrease cortisol, which is tied to stress, depression, and anxiety. It boosts our immune system, and releases feel-good neurochemicals including oxytocin, a hormone that is also called the love or cuddle hormone that plays an important part in feelings of pleasure and our sense of well-being. Studies confirm that babies who do not get hugged do not develop normally.

For the next month, incorporate more hugging in your life and experiment with making your hugs longer, more intentional, and more present. The average hug is only three seconds so work your way up to a therapeutic 20 and think of it as charging your battery, or giving someone a healthy boost. Hug a person so that their head is to the left of yours and both of your hearts connect.

With the right people in your life, it will feel appropriate. If you realize you are hug-avoidant, abstain for now and instead, journal on beliefs, fears, or past trauma that may hinder your willingness to experiment with your sense of touch.

Receiving and giving hugs is the most powerful way to get and show support.

18. Love Thy Engine— Diesel & Spine

Align your Body

"A mechanic of the heart knows how to harmonize with the spine." —Carole

Eric complained, "It's so freaking hot my eyeballs are sweating." His drenched bandana confirming it.

He tried to squeeze his 6'2" frame inside the engine room, a small crawling space of about 5' x 12' located underneath the cockpit floor and crammed with stacked bins of spare parts for our boat. The space was made even smaller by our oversized 85hp Perkins 4-236 diesel motor that the previous owner had installed leaving barely enough room to maneuver. It left maybe four feet around him to move and make repairs.

It was accessible from the hallway, and we temporarily removed the small doors to give him a few extra inches to wiggle but his legs were sticking out. I sat beside him, both knees against the sides of the passageway calling out numbers.

"Number 12", reading off a chart he gave me, "12," he replied, looking for the correlating number he had marked on top of the engine to identify the 22 bolts that he needed to tighten. The torque pattern wasn't linear and created a crisscross spiderweb that slowly tightened the top of the engine and head gasket in a precise way. Eric used his wrench to torque the #12 head bolt until he heard the click. We moved on to the next, keeping count, and going through the sequence up to 22, and starting the pattern over and over until all 22 had been torqued with equal amounting pressure to seal the head gasket thoroughly.

Not all days on a sailboat were spent sunbathing or watching dolphins play. Some were done in dark, diesel-smelling corners, with no air and no room to move, but it had to be done. *If you wanna play, you gotta pay!*

After step one, he moved to adjusting the valves which was another precise operation where he rotated the engine while watching the rocker arm on the valve and adjusted it. Everything he did was to the hundredths of millimeters. It's remarkable how man created machines that move so fast, with so much power, and under so much pressure—all while being aligned into a space smaller than a hair. All this functions inside a boat, while being shaken every which way when underway. I was grateful for this bad boy who pulled us out of many jams over the years. It deserved our respect, along with the mechanic who cared for it, too!

By the time Eric was done and crawled out of the small space, he had spent hours contorted around the engine. When he tried to stand, he had a hard time unfolding his frame. We high-fived as he achingly stretched and celebrated checking off this huge job from his to-do list. Bolts, valves, shaft, and motor were aligned. The captain required a few days of rest for his spine to get back in line, but Windsong had its iron sail back.

LESSON: Align your body

When I hurt my neck in a serious accident and ended with a neck brace for months while doing intense physical therapy, I realized how important spine alignment was in a sailor's life. I couldn't winch, lift, coil, and barely threw a dock line. My engine was broken, and I was deadweight.

Eric also dealt with back issues where doctors wanted to do a spinal fusion–a major surgery fusing vertebrae with a metal plate. He refused, choosing to put his trust in our friend, Scott, an expert acupuncturist who worked diligently for months on both of us to help ease our pain so that our bodies could tap into their healing ability. I also practiced yoga and stretched every day to help my spine regain its flexibility and keep it healthy.

When the spine loses its alignment, not only does it hurt, but it disturbs the flow of energy in our meridians and chakras. Injuries are more than physical—they are energetic as well. Both are important to care for. So, when I started therapy to heal my spine, I also learned to care for my body's energy to ease my pain and promote faster healing.

Strengthening my core and being conscientious of my alignment have been key in rehabilitation. I flow through life with a better posture, stronger in my stance, energizing my body, chakras, and my brain. Didn't you know? A healthy spine is scientifically proven to improve cognitive functions! [7] [8]

QUESTION: What does my body need to be in alignment?

ACTION: Heart posture

A super simple tip to help with posture is to never cross your arms in front of you, rather, cross them in the back. That way, you are expanding the ribcage and shoulders, allowing your heart to lift and open while straightening the spine. Line up the back of your skull with your sacrum and activate your navel for best alignment. (Thanks to the incredible Iyengar teacher, Yogarosa in Hallandale, Florida, for this valuable tip that I've been using for 18 years!)

19. Feast on Self-Love— For Gut's Sake

Align Nutrition and your Gut

> *"A faulty lighthouse never helped anyone."*
> —Carole

My year of convalescing was tough. The years of surgeries, illness, and physical and emotional stress had taken a toll on me and I was trying to put it all behind.

I had never put any thoughts into my "American" diet or the provisions in my pantry, until I learned how intrinsically connected my nutrition was to my health. In fact, it was everything.

My amazing functional medicine doctor who figured out what was wrong with me by performing a DNA test* after I fired my many Western medicine doctors, helped me realign my nutrition with my gut.

With my new gluten-free, dairy-free, no sugar, no nightshades, no red meat, no alcohol, or caffeine diet I wasn't constantly sick anymore. But heck, was I struggling to stay the course!

Who wouldn't after eating 21 days of bland white rice, (complex carbs were discouraged and too difficult to digest at the time; doctor's order), chicken or fish, and only certain low-sugar fruits and steamed veggies. Goodbye sauces, creams, butter, sweets, and cheeses.

I knew I needed to heal my digestive system, and goodness, I was ready to feel well. I had 40+ years of eating habits to transition.

Anyone who's made the New Year's resolution of losing a few pounds knows how, by February (even January), common it is to slide back into their old habits, sneaking treats and telling themselves, "Just this once!"

Since Eric still ate a "normal" diet, I could not simply stop buying the foods on my NO list, and temptation was sometimes greater than my resolve.

My palate starved for flavor. Part of the problem was that I had not found equally satisfying alternatives to replace my favorite food items, so I reverted to foods that pleased my taste buds.

I had huge, almost uncontrollable cravings for chocolate which regrettably always resulted in flare-ups. I was given a large list of foods that I could not eat anymore—some for a minimum of one year, some for the rest of my life. This new nutrition plan stripped away part of my French identity: CHEESE!

I would feel amazing for a few weeks, even months, almost forgetting that I used to be sick when I ate certain things. Hoping my stomach and DNA miraculously changed, a tiny little bit of cheddar would find its way onto my plate—oh boy, I'd be lying on the couch for a week damning my weakness.

I wished I had access to a nutritionist but could not afford it, so I relied on my doctor's recommendations and my own research. I educated myself but struggled with accountability. A food coach would have helped make the process smoother and more efficient. I have a policy of living with no regrets, so it is what it is.

I worked on being gentle and encouraged myself when I "fell off the wagon." It took a long time but eventually, my cravings subsided, and I developed a new palate.

The more I healed my gut, the more I learned to listen to my body, and the more I healed my relationship with it. I rebuilt the trust I had in a body that failed me for the last few years.

Or was it I who had failed it by not paying attention to the signs it was giving me and disconnecting myself from my gut feelings? I had turned away from the pain but had not heeded its warnings, or acted on its valuable messages.

I could not heal if I was disconnected. So, I dove in, nourished my body, balanced my gut, and learned to feast on self-love.

LESSON: Align nutrition and your gut

Be wary of the little brain hackers living in your stomach! When you take antibiotics, and medication, eat a diet of processed or sugary foods, drink caffeine and alcohol, etc., you harm the sensitive ecosystem residing in your gut, known as the "microbiome." When it is out of balance, some of the good bacteria and fungi fall prey to the invasive ones, which multiply and cause all kinds of health issues—some very serious.

After my first car accident, I took doctor-prescribed antibiotics, anti-inflammatories, and pain medicine for relief. Six months later, I ended up at my primary care physician with my stomach flora destroyed and a list of complaints. He ran a Candida test suspecting invasive candidiasis, but the test came back as a false negative–which blood tests sometimes do. I never questioned the original test until my functional medicine doctor mentioned the possibility years later and asked that more thorough testing be done which changed my life.* I knew in my gut (no pun intended) that my stomach was key to healing but sadly, I doubted myself more than I doubted my doctors.

The flourishing case of *Candida albicans* overgrowth was not the only culprit but it did perform a lot of damage and some health practitioners speculated it started the chain reaction that activated dormant Celiac as well as my gluten-sensitive genes, lactose intolerance, dyspepsia, leaky gut, and chronic inflammation that all followed. This string of dis-ease overloaded all bodily systems and indirectly caused my hysterectomy, hemorrhoidectomy, and lesions on my liver. (These little buggers are rabble-rousers!)

Educating myself on the subject, I learned that these microorganisms need sugar to thrive and send signals to our brain asking for sweets and carbs which are metabolized into glucose. We interpret those as cravings and respond by eating candy, pizzas, sodas, etc., when it's actually the bacteria running the ship. REALLY! They even affect our moods and behaviors! Yikes!!

Who's in charge here?

Since then, every time I crave something I ask myself if I am truly hungry or under the influence of bacteria. This awareness makes it easier to avoid the bag of chips and has put me back in the driver's seat.

Get the mutiny under control by eating wholesome foods and watch your cravings disappear. It might take a few weeks but stick with it and you will soon feel energized, think more clearly, and you'll super-charge your immune system!

Plus, our gut is also in charge of sending internal cues from our environment to our brain, but if we let the mutineers take over, it cannot do its job properly, diminishing our intuition, and our capacity to function in the world.

Chapter 19 — Align Nutrition and your Gut

Finally, the health of our microbiome affects our mental health. Read that again.

Energetically, nourishment is associated with our first or root chakra which relates to all earthly and physical things. It is where we get our stability in the physical world. It is important to feed ourselves wholesome, organic, high-energy foods. Digestion is associated with our third chakra, the solar plexus, so a healthy power center is as important to avoid digestive issues, or blockages.

Didn't think you had stowaways onboard, did you? Hope this helps motivate you in keeping your crew in check for when you need to be at your best!

QUESTION: The next time I have a gut feeling I will...

ACTION: Produce galore

I challenge you for the next month (or three!), every time you provision and grocery shop:

1) Buy fruits and produce you have never (or rarely) eaten

2) Eat every color of the rainbow

3) Double the amount of greens on your plate

4) Add foods that are filled with natural probiotics like kimchi, sauerkraut, apple cider vinegar, etc., to your diet

5) When taking antibiotics or prescription medicine, add a probiotic supplement to your diet.**

The more variety and color in each meal, the more tantalizing a bounty you visually connect with and the healthier your gut will be.

*(see book 1)

**The information contained in this book is meant to educate and in no way intended to provide medical advice. We encourage readers to seek professional help for any and all health conditions.

20. Three Sheets to the Wind—A Rebel Crew

Align Communications with your Heart

"I couldn't heal because I kept pretending I wasn't hurt."
—*Unknown*

Dictionary: To be "three sheets to the wind" is to be drunk. The sheet is the line that controls the sails on a ship. If the line is not secured, the sail flops in the wind, and the ship loses headway and control. If all three sails are loose, the ship is out of control.

Part 1—My awakening

I could feel him falling off the edge and did not know how to reach him or what to do about it.

That old saying, "Let's talk about the elephant in the room" came to mind, about there being something so obvious yet so shadowed that you don't want to discuss it. Well, we sailed with a wild bull elephant in the cabin. It had a penchant for rum and was so heavy that the floorboards cracked under pressure and salt water stained the teak. Our foundation was threatened. When the elephant overindulged, it was rowdy, loud, obnoxious—and almost sank our relationship.

When floating surrounded by water, it's impossible to escape something threatening your peace. Thankfully, this elephant was tamed at sea. But when we docked, and often around the full moon (the myth is true), it came out like a wild boar, crushing our peace, howling at the moon, making it difficult to navigate life in a marina (society) and act civilized. There wasn't enough room aboard our 41' footer for me and a raging elephant. We were bound for troubled waters.

Eric's mental health has been a constant up and down his whole life. He started self-medicating at a young age—probably to numb his highly sensitive nature—and came from a family that lacked communication and coping skills, instead they reached for alcohol. Emotional displays were frowned upon, and family traumas were hidden away, never to be dealt with. So, despite his heart being in pain, he did not know how to express or heal it. The louder it cried, the more he numbed it. The heart will keep sending signals until it is acknowledged.

His doctor had put him on Lexapro (for anxiety and depression) since his last burnout two years prior when he quit his job, and we had sailed south. New horizons, new discoveries, and new destinations had only temporarily postponed the inevitable—diving within was the only way to slay the imaginary monsters. Despite his panic attacks being mostly under control, he struggled with anxiety disorder and had been drinking heavily for a while as a deterrent. I saw signs that he was on a slippery slope.

The only time I saw him relax was when we sailed away. Life on land seemed to raise his anxiety but we did not have the resources to completely cut off until the boat was paid off. He was professionally accomplished and rarely let it affect his work, but at night, happy hour at the marina often got out of control.

Following the discovery of liver lesions while being treated for my auto-immune disease, I was now completely sober. I was training in health and wellness to heal myself, and he was spiraling into his destructive habits. He resisted any and all advice from the now "sober wife." I don't think he felt that he had a problem and my prying only

Chapter 20 — Align Communications with your Heart

made things worse. We were completely out of alignment with each other. I worried. I know that he felt it too, and it scared him.

Drained from my dark night of the soul, and on the mend, I found solace in yoga and meditation. This was so out of character for me and foreign to Eric. He had no idea what was happening to his wife. All he saw was that the more classes I attended, the happier I was, and he supported that, but he also saw me change, pull away, and start to explore life without him.

Worried that there wouldn't be a place for him in Carole 2.0's life, he also felt stuck because we hadn't sailed much while I recuperated and regained my strength. He was afraid of losing me and being left behind, which brought up fear of abandonment from his past. He drank to cope with the stress.

Of course you can imagine this only made things worse because I pulled away even more. Alcohol traps more people than just the person who drinks. The more he drank, the more frustrated and angry I got, and the angrier I got, the more he drank, it was a vicious cycle.

I felt terribly unhappy, uncertain about our future, and without the emotional strength to tackle this new crisis. I was just starting to figure out my own stuff and worried about his state of mind. We had both been through a lot and needed to find our way back.

We landed in a small marina where slips were tight, and people were allowed to work on their boats. The place doubled as a boatyard where half the slips were for boats being refurbished and the other slips were for transient boaters and liveaboards. It had direct access to the ocean so crewed yachts up to 145' could come in and get work done. It was noisy and dusty on the weekdays but our low budget and their open policy to work on your boat was perfect timing to do some sanding, buffing, and painting on Windsong.

Most marinas have a low tolerance for certain types of work on your boat with rules to keep it tidy and noise-free. Windsong needed some TLC, and we could refurbish it without annoying the neighborhood. It was time to get me and Windsong back in shape.

Eric had been in a dark mood for months. I'm sure supporting me through my sickness and worrying about my health, then seeing me distance away was taxing. It was time to raise the red flag on Windsong because I was at a loss on how or where to get help.

Serendipitously, a few weeks later, two of our closest friends arrived bags in tow. Their vacation was planned just when Windsong's crew was in dire need of assistance.

It was a rough landing. For the first few days, my capitaine was completely unhinged, drinking and partying more than they'd ever seen him even in his rowdy past. On the third day, his friends asked me, "What the hell is going on?" and the floodgates opened.

It's a tough situation to discuss sensitive family issues. You don't want people to judge or change the way they treat you or your loved ones, you don't want to embarrass yourself or your spouse—whom you love dearly—and try to be strong and hold it together but after a while you get lost in a gray cloud of toxic patterns, triggers, and excuses. It's hard to realize how bad things are because you've lived in it for so long that you've somewhat become desensitized to mayhem.

I had been so focused on helping him, healing him, fixing him, controlling his drinking, and holding it together that I silenced my own feelings. Once I started talking, I couldn't stop. It felt like a huge weight being lifted off my shoulders. I admitted that our lives had become unmanageable.

That night, his friend tried to talk to him. It was a disastrous night. I'd never seen him in such bad shape, and I don't think his friends had either. He was out of control and very unkind. I apologized to his friends

Chapter 20 — Align Communications with your Heart

and went to bed. I was on board a sinking ship and drowning. I heard them go on for hours (a 41' boat is very small). My hubby was a rebel, there was no way he was going to sleep, he felt like partying even if he couldn't hold it together anymore. His buddy waited for hours to go to bed until he passed out.

The following day his best friends told me: "When he's like this, you need to get out, you need to leave. You need to shock him out of it, pack your bags, and go take care of yourself. That may be the only thing that snaps him out of this downward spiral and saves him."

When I heard this coming from his best friend, it broke the spell and brought me back to reality. I had been sailing in thick fog. So accustomed to yo-yoing with this disease for years that I had not realized how toxic the situation had become. I was losing him, and he was losing me.

They went out to lunch. I don't know what was said, all I know is that I can pinpoint to this day a profound shift in my husband. That's when the first rays of light pierced through the clouds, and I recognized my husband behind those baby blue eyes again. He was there. He was listening. There was hope.

The following week our friends left, and we talked and shared what we had been feeling, and what we wanted for the future, reassuring, and listening to each other's hopes and fears.

This was the match. The naughty party was the explosion.

Part 2—His awakening

It all started because a guy peed off the dock. The mega yacht was so high that from the top deck looking down, the deckhand on it assumed that the sailor was relieving himself on their hull, when in fact, due to the curvature of the boat, the hull was well over 5 feet away from the dock.

The dock party went late into the night and the yacht had the unfortunate luck of floating next to the community tiki where boaters gathered after hours. The deckhand's anger escalated and prompted his first bad decision of the night—he walked down the gangway and stepped off the boat.

He went straight into the face of the sailor he thought he saw peeing on his hull and shouted accusations. By now, the sailor had long since stashed away the tool of the crime and explained the deckhand's skewed line of sight and miscalculation. But the yachtie was arrogant and adamant about, "putting this drunken sailor into place." Words heated; F-bombs dropped. One of the sailor's friends got up, a petite woman with enough bravery to shush any guy. She stepped in between the two to calm things down, just as the deckhand stretched back and threw a punch.

His second bad decision of the night—he hit a girl. Someone's girl. A girl who had the unfortunate timing of inserting herself in the conversation just as the punch flew. A girl whose man was 100% muscles and wound up on Tequila and had no qualms about kicking this fine-suited ass, to valiantly protect his girl.

That someone entrusted his guitar to Eric and said, "Protect my guitar, man," as he jumped up to save the woman he loved.

Of course, the girlfriend screamed and got hurt, and chaos ensued. The men started to brawl. Fists flew and he took the scallywag down. Her boyfriend was way more able to defend himself than anyone in the crowd; the altercation didn't need any more men jumping in. Sailors on the dock watched the crew members on deck and nervous tempers filled the air. No one wanted the fight to escalate but everyone was chiming in.

Eric, who had been behaving all night decided that it was enough craziness for him. The guitar still in hand, he left the scene of the crime and walked down the dock leaving mayhem behind. When he climbed down below and told me what happened, I was stunned. This is not how tiki parties at marinas typically end. In fact, it was the only time in 20 years that we'd seen this.

Just then, red and blue flashing lights illuminated our faces. We looked out the portholes and saw police cruisers fill the darkness. Oy vey! Someone had called 5-0 and they were taking in our two friends and the deckhand for booking. That sailor probably wished he had kept it in his pants!

Within a week, we raised sails. This explosion woke my captain up and he was fully engaged with me again. The wall between us broke down and it was us against the world again. We made plans to sail out of the area and reclaim our future.

LESSON: Align your communications with your heart

Miscommunications happen because of so many reasons but the underlying theme is almost always that we are:

1) not listening to others

2) not listening to ourselves

I was part of the problem. I enabled. I only spoke up to nag. I wasn't listening to what was NOT being said. I missed his fears, hints, and body language—all were lost behind my frustrations, expectations, and desire to control situations. Instead of communicating with compassion and understanding, I was stuck in anger and frustration.

When I spoke, I was aligned with my fears and the stories playing in my mind, so my ego took charge and reacted in ways I was not proud of. Even the most peaceful people can be assholes sometimes and say mean things. I was, and I did. I threw fuel on a fiery situation.

When I took inventory of my life, fears, and feelings, I felt the hurt behind our actions and how misaligned we were. We let fears steer our relationship and love took a back seat. Once I understood this, I started shifting my conversations and aligning my words with my heart, overlooking the judgments cast by my ego. I focused on gratefulness and hope.

I caught my tongue more than a few times, breathing and dropping into my heart, then connecting before talking.

Love became the guiding force. Eric felt it and with all that happened, he was ready to listen. The more I loved and forgave him—and myself—the more compassionate I was toward him, and the more he opened up about his feelings and started to take better care of himself.

Our hearts were aligning again! We found ourselves hand-in-hand in the eye of the storm where before he was spinning behind a wall of chaos and noise, unable to hear me.

He realized that we needed to save our ship—our relation-ship—and we both put efforts into it.

You can't tell me that any 30-year relationship hasn't sailed through tough times where one might have considered, even for a second, leaving their spouse. Let's get real, relationships are HARD. It takes a lot more than Valentine's roses to last through decades in any partnership, and still feel excited about the future. It takes heart-to-heart conversations.

Chapter 20 — Align Communications with your Heart

We talked a lot in the following months and smoothed out many problems. Our throat chakras were activated, and I was adamant about keeping mine aligned and flowing with my heart. This new way of navigating troubled waters saved us.

I am also forever grateful for friend-ships—the ships of friends who came to our rescue and helped us course-correct. Mindfulness, journaling, and 12-step recovery programs for family members also helped me simplify the drama in my head all gave me tools to communicate what I was feeling without being triggered or having it turned into arguments. I learned that I was powerless over someone's addictions or mental conditions. I could only be responsible for myself. I became mindful of what was driving my conversations and how I was communicating with others. My heart became a compass.

There are support groups and 12-step programs (like Al-Anon) to help family members of loved ones struggling with issues. It can be a lifeline; they offer free services in most cities and everywhere with internet access. Don't be afraid to ask for help. These are amazingly welcoming tribes ready to help you out of the storm.

Opening the door to higher communications helped me engage an emotional intelligence that could resolve conflicts without being triggered, listen without feeling targeted, and help without feeling defeated.

The clouds around us dissipated and we felt a renewed love for each other and zest for life.

QUESTION: What is making me angry that I'm not saying?

ACTION: Balancing breath (alternate nostril breathing, aka *Nadi Shodhanana*)

Did you know that at any given time of the day, we only breathe through one nostril at a time?

Each nostril is connected to the opposite side of the brain and body's energy channels.

A great way to calm yourself before having a stressful conversation or when tension runs high is through a technique called alternate nostril breathing. It helps regulate your nervous system, lower your blood pressure, and balance your energy—and your brain—so that you can ground yourself and communicate from a peaceful center. As you practice this breath, you raise your level of awareness and can better manage your feelings.

Sit in a comfortable position and turn your attention inward. Close your eyes, be present, and notice your breath. Use your right thumb to close your right nostril and inhale deeply through the left nostril. Pause, swing the right index finger over to close the left nostril, and exhale through the right nostril. Inhale through the right nostril, pause, close your right nostril, exhale deeply through the left nostril, and continue breathing through alternate nostrils for 3 to 5 minutes. You'll experience instant relaxation as both hemispheres of the brain become balanced. This is very soothing for the nervous system. It will balance both sides of the brain and turn on the parasympathetic nervous system which manages our "rest and digest" functions. It is also a great revitalizer that helps enhance mental function, sharpens your focus, calms overacting minds, and brings better sleep.

Throughout the day, practice noticing which side you are breathing from and intentionally changing it!

Conclusion

Align with Purpose

Sailing into the unknown!

> *"Dear unknown, I embrace you with hope, be gentle as I fill my sails with courage."* —Carole

The incredible feeling of finally being free of my fears overwhelmed me with tremendous joy.

I was regaining my health and my husband, and finally felt excited about work again. I had found a great source of inner strength that I did not know I possessed. With it came the feeling of connection and being aligned with every step I was taking. All that did not serve me anymore was drifting away, replaced by feelings of lightness and inspiration. What was this sparkling feeling I sensed all over my body—like little love bubbles percolating in total happiness? WOW. I had not felt inspired in too many years.

I turned, looked back at my husband at the helm to see he was also beaming with joy. After some time refurbishing our cruising kitty and planning our future, our minds and hearts were clear and aligned. We said our goodbyes to friends (tears were shed!), quit our jobs and sailed away from our regular sailing stomping ground for the very last time.

In front of us was a world of possibilities. It felt exhilarating and I wanted to shout **HOPE LIVES** out to the world! Somehow I needed to broadcast a message to anyone going through tough times to hang on, and reach out! If I could sail through it and feel THIS amazingly well, surely, they could do it, too!

I survived the doldrums, turbulent waters, dark storms, and desperation, yet I felt uplifted, and invisibly guided toward a better future. A great sense of purpose animated my heart and somehow, in some way, I would share all that I had learned to help others find their North Star.

I smiled at my irresistible husband, delighted we crossed the last bridge to land together. Up ahead, the great unknown. We would face it together.

I stood on the bow of Windsong and felt the depth of my heart flood with gratitude. Tears welled in my eyes for this second lease on life, for this moment in time. I was committing to memory this man who stood beside me, through thick and thin, having found my way to spirit, and this blue horizon opening in front of me. I embraced it all.

I opened my arms as wide as I could and shouted, "FREEDOM!!!" Eric busted out laughing.

I felt saltwater spray splash over my face and licked my lips giggling. It felt great to be alive. I was more than happy; I was sailing above the clouds.

LESSON: Align with purpose

There is magic in aligning and clearing away all that does not feel *right*. Guidance was part of my soul, and I could finally hear and feel it. I had to share my story. I wanted to help others. I needed to write our story. I felt magnetized by this idea because our adventures held such wisdom for me, I was convinced others would benefit from them too. We all deserve to hear the whispers of our souls.

Whatever you do and wherever you are, may you radiate your soul's energy into all that you do to realize and appreciate your full potential!

QUESTION: What does my head want?
What does my heart want?
What does my spirit want?

 ACTION: Align to shine!

Carefully weigh your answers to the questions above, and all that you have learned about your passion and motivation in the exercises.

Every choice, action, and decision either brings you closer or farther away from your purpose.

- What your spirit wants is alignment with purpose
- What your heart wants is alignment with joy
- What your mind wants is more complex because it is governed by your ego which is often aligned with limiting beliefs, fears, and misplaced motivations. However, it manages logistics and your relations in the world. What it really wants is to be mastered! In so doing, it will work to support your goals

Align all three and you will feel energized, inspired, and shine through every endeavor!

THE END...

SNEAK PEEK

S.A.I.L. Above the Clouds Book #3—Integrate Tools for Success

We felt Windsong veer violently into the wind—we had just lost our anchor and the ferocious storm took us hostage. We dropped everything and ran on deck. Eric rushed to the bow, grabbed the spare anchor, shackled it and threw it into the raging bay while I started the engine and motored us at maximum speed against the wind. We were sailing sideways skimming across the chop, captured by the invisible force. Through the pouring rain, we saw a neighboring boat in the same predicament. Helpless, we watched it drift out of control and crash into the island's mangroves. Yeeeouch.

We turned to see Mom and Dad's worried faces peeking in the cockpit. "It's going to be a long night" we told them. "The storm is here."

WHAT'S AHEAD?!

BOOK #3 is jam-packed with adventures where I learned to **INTEGRATE TOOLS FOR SUCCESS.** It's one thing to feel good and excited when embarking on a journey but how can we sustain our enthusiasm, focus, and inspiration, day in and day out?

Learn how to integrate the lessons, develop, and instill beneficial habits and forge healthy ways of thinking that emphasize your actions, and anchor the practices so that they support you through life, and you remain INSPIRED despite storms and wild adventures.

You'll adventure into the times when:
- We alllllllmost sank, miles away from civilization

- Windsong's 50-foot mast needed major heeling to slide under a low bridge

- Stormy seas brought my mom to a near heart attack

- Windsong dragged anchor in a surprise gale

- I became witness to a man's last hour after a violent suicide (turned trauma into gratitude)

- Furry crew members stole the spotlight

- A shocking truth bomb was dropped

If you are wondering how to manifest your vision and reach your goal, this book will help you explore how to integrate tools for better relationships, build the discipline necessary to accomplish your goals, and establish a daily practice that supports your growth. If you're not using the tools in your treasure box, you won't be able to sustain an abundant healthy lifestyle.

What's Ahead?

In BOOK #4, I share about surviving the doldrums of a 30-year relationship on board a 41-foot vessel, sailing into alligator land, being chased naked by a shark, the quest for no tan lines, and sinking a dinghy, leaving us stranded on a deserted beach. I will recount the scariest day we've had on Windsong in 25 years. To give you a sneak peek, this was when we sailed up the East Coast from Florida to Maine and got caught in a dangerous 3.5-hour gale storm. We almost lost control of the boat, completely trashed it, almost caught fire, and I ended up having to abandon ship with a dorsal sprain—alone in a strange town. This forced me to dig deep, to survive the heartbreak of moving off Windsong halfway through our trip in an unknown town. Here, I found myself homeless with my bags on the curb, hurt, and alone. I had to find the strength to **LET GO** and trust that life would find a miraculous way of bringing Eric, me, and Windsong back together, to make everything alright again. I will also divulge a huge family secret I'd been carrying around for years.

Letting go is the ultimate act of freedom. It is the hardest thing to do, but the key to blissful peace and happiness. If you are experiencing resistance in any aspect of your life, there is something that needs to be **LET GO**. Read this book and try the exercises to help you achieve a level of surrender that will benefit your whole wellbeing. In learning to trust yourself, you will gain a whole new level of self-acceptance and fulfillment.

FREEBIES

Visit SailAboveTheClouds.com and download your FREE powerful chakra chart to help you in your quest for alignment.

...and don't forget to download your FREE meditation!

Use CODE: 1111

SailAboveTheClouds.com

Please review this book!

Reviews help authors more than you might think. If you enjoyed *SAIL Above the Clouds*, please consider leaving a review at your Amazon or regular bookstore—it would be greatly appreciated—and may help Carole's stories sail towards unknown horizons!

...please share it with your friends...

About The Author

Carole sailed from Florida to Maine where she currently lives with her husband of 33-years. She enjoys discovering the vast nature that New England offers. She is a successful professional graphic designer, and continues her life-long study of holistic and yogic philosophies and learning ways of managing her health.

Carole is a certified Life Coach, Meditative Writing, Shakti Dance® Yoga, and Reiki Master Teacher. She teaches stress-relief, mindfulness, yoga, and meditative writing. She coaches and mentors women of all ages who seek inspiration and positive energy, so they can be proactive towards healing their bodies and minds to lead purposeful and healthier lives.

Find out more at Inspiredlifebycarole.com and sign up for her newsletter for free helpful tips, life hacks, stories, and meditations.

Say Hello!

You can connect with Carole in a number of places. She inspires people on Facebook, through writing and uplifting shares, she visually entices on Instagram, she reviews and recommends her favorite books on Good Reads, and you can send her an email too. She welcomes your correspondence and will answer you personally.

Email: sailabovetheclouds@gmail.com
Facebook: @InspiredCreationsInc & Inspired Life By Carole
Instagram: @inspiredlifebycarole
Threads: @inspiredlifebycarole
TikTok: @inspiredlifebycarole

References

[1] Madhav Goyal, MD, MPH1; Sonal Singh, MD, MPH1; Erica M. S. Sibinga, MD, MHS2, March 2014, *Meditation Programs for Psychological Stress and Well-being - A Systematic Review and Meta-analysis,* JAMA Network.

[2] Eileen Luders, Nicolas Cherbuin, and Florian Kurth, F*orever Young(er): potential age-defying effects of long-term meditation on gray matter atrophy,* 21 January 2015, Frontiers in Psychology.

[3] Judson A. Brewer, Patrick D. Worhunsky, Jeremy R. Gray, Yi-Yuan Tang, Jochen Weber, and Hedy Kober, December 13, 2011, *Meditation experience is associated with differences in default mode network activity and connectivity,* Proceedings of the National Academy of Sciences of the United States of America.

[4] McManus DE. *Reiki Is Better Than Placebo and Has Broad Potential as a Complementary Health Therapy.* J Evid Based Complementary Altern Med. 2017 Oct;22(4):1051-1057. doi: 10.1177/2156587217728644. Epub 2017 Sep 5. PMID: 28874060; PMCID: PMC5871310.

[5] *Stars and Planets,* Ian Ridpath, Eyewitness Handbook, DK Publishing.

[6] Howard E. LeWine, MD, *Oxytocin: The love hormone,* Harvard Health Publishing, June 13, 2023.
-*Why Hugging Is Actually Good for Your Health*—Cleveland Clinic, health.clevelandclinic.org, October 21, 2020
-Erica Cirino, *Why You Should Get (and Give) More Hugs,* healthline.com, April 11, 2018.

[7] @srinipillay, *The psychology of low back pain,* Harvard Health Publishing, April 25, 2016

[8] National Library of Medicine, Carrick FR. *Changes in brain function after manipulation of the cervical spine.* J Manipulative Physiol Ther. 1997 Oct;20(8):529-45. Erratum in: J Manipulative Physiol Ther 1998 May;21(4):304. PMID: 9345682.

Resources

Al-anon.org: Worldwide support for family members concerned about a loved one with a drinking problem.

Insighttimer.com: Free guided meditation and discussions Follow me @inspiredcarole

Nami.org: National Alliance on Mental Illness, USA's largest grassroots mental health organization dedicated to building better lives for millions of Americans affected by mental illness.

Samhsa.gov: USA's National Helpline, a free, confidential, 24/7, 365-day-a-year treatment referral and information service (in English and Spanish) for individuals and families facing mental and/or substance use disorders. 1-800-662-HELP (4357).

Science of Mind: Monthly magazine, scienceofmind.com.

Stars and Planets, Ian Ridpath, Eyewitness Handbook, DK Publishing.

Journaling

www.ingramcontent.com/pod-product-compliance
Lightning Source LLC
Chambersburg PA
CBHW071225080526
44587CB00013BA/1501